Anna Wilkes

Ireland

Ur of the Chaldees

Anna Wilkes

Ireland
Ur of the Chaldees

ISBN/EAN: 9783337322496

Printed in Europe, USA, Canada, Australia, Japan

Cover: Foto ©ninafisch / pixelio.de

More available books at **www.hansebooks.com**

IRELAND:

UR OF THE CHALDEES.

BY

ANNA WILKES.

LONDON:

Published for the Author by

TRÜBNER & CO., LUDGATE HILL.

1873.

ERRATA.

For	*page*		*read*
For Semetic,	*page* xvii, &c.	*read*	Semitic.
,, Ashkenez,	,, xx and 62,	,,	Ashkenaz.
,, Togamah,	,, xx and 63,	,,	Togarmah.
,, Eboricum,	,, xxii, 40, 106, 108	,,	Eboracum.
,, Jocktan,	,, xxii, 112, 115, 121	,,	Joktan.
,, Therapuetes,	,, xxiii,	,,	Therapeutes.
,, Guibelines,	,, xxiv, 191,	,,	Ghibelines.
,, Attay,	,, 10,	,,	Altaï.
,, Italian,	,, 19,	,,	Latin.
,, Ἶταλος,	,, 19,	,,	Γίταλος.
,, Aram Naharam,	,, 27, 103, 124,	,,	Aram Naharaim.
,, Midian,	,, 32,	,,	Madian.
,, Gallacia	,, 41,	,,	Gallicia.
,, Mane Lud,	,, 42,	,,	Mané Lud.
,, Dodanam,	,, 64,	,,	Dodanim.
,, Haram,	,, 68,	,,	Haran.
,, Isaiah,	,, 71,	,,	Uzziah.
,, Midian,	,, 78,	,,	Madian.
,, Arimespians,	,, 103,	,,	Arimaspians.
,, Salesbury,	,, 105,	,,	Salisbury.
,, *Oanes,*	,, 108,	,,	*Oännes.*
,, Essinians,	,, 109,	,,	Essenians.
,, Cladius,	,, 113,	,,	Claudius.
,, Charron,	,, 148,	,,	Charran.
,, Bœtius,	,, 122, 172,	,,	Boëtius.
,, Geskie,	,, 179,	,,	Geikie.
,, Ramsey,	,, 181,	,,	Ramsay.
,, Sier,	,, 186,	,,	Seir.
,, Higgin's,	,, 206,	,,	Higgins'.

PREFACE.

THE material that has engaged my attention in the following pages is principally taken from the Mosaic, the Koran, Talmud, and Celtic references to the first peoples and places.

As far as possible I have avoided loading the subject with technical terms and problems to be met with in Anthropology—a science necessarily contributing considerable matter to the text—but have preferred to use in it history, tradition, folk-lore, and other interests that go towards a proof that the *first* human families must have migrated from the west of Europe to Asia, and *not* from Asia to the west of Europe.

This may appear strange to some people; but it will occur to the reflecting and intelligent mind that it is quite possible to do over again, some of the work of Scripture commentators and interpreters, and be at the same time, in perfect harmony with the Bible. For instance, the sites of the *principal* countries, cities, and places mentioned in that book, are by their own confession, up to the present, *unascertained.* Therefore the necessity existed for re-considering the *teachings of men*, as distinguished from the lessons of the Bible, which, for my part, are accepted as correct and veracious.

In the following pages there is no allusion to the doctrine of " Independent development," but they admit that human beings multiplied from a *first pair.*

As far as I know, I have not offended the prejudices of any people or creed. In making much reference to the first inhabitants of the British Islands, there has been an endeavour to show that a great deal of the past—the pre-historic as well as the historic past—is marked by their actions. From this it is advised, that their descendants, as well as those esteeming themselves of Saxon, Danish, or Norman blood, should remove the race asperities that so frequently operate against one another, and join with the Celt in mutual respect and prosperity.

Because thousands of years have passed away with man, and the correct register of his first existence and efforts here—so, like others, but not in a general way,—I have felt obliged to labour, and to particularise, and bring together, out of the confused yet evident relationship of primeval man, the similarities of his thoughts as they are written, of his speech as it is known, and of the signs that endure from his chisel and pen.

How I have succeeded in this is now to be

judged by my critics. It may be the task I have undertaken will appear to them too difficult for the grasp of woman's mind. That it has been difficult I willingly confess, and perhaps the pages will indicate this more than I am conscious of. They are, however, the product of years of reading and reflection, and as such have been thought worthy of publication.

Whether this book be or not successful—and its success cannot be reckoned by its completeness—there are such quantities of like material yet unused, that it will be at no distant date drawn upon and put forth in a periodical.

I cannot allow this volume to go to the world without expressing my sincere and heartfelt acknowledgments of the ready and kind assistance that I have never ceased to receive from my husband throughout the whole of my work and investigations. His constant reading of Biblical history—his profound and unalterable faith in that Book of books, has enabled me to supplement, to illustrate, and to enforce my convictions on the subject which I have undertaken, whilst his devotion to the cause we have both at heart, rendered his suggestions doubly valuable, and more than doubly welcome.

ANNA WILKES.

UPPER NORWOOD,
September, 1873.

INTRODUCTION.

PERHAPS nothing is more characteristic of the present age than the advances made from all quarters in the cause of truth. Dogma, as well as theory, is subjected to the investigations of the thoughtful; and nothing is allowed to pass as true without bearing its full complement of laudation and abuse. Facts often make their appearance with unwinning surroundings, and it is not until they have stood their proper time under examination that they are admitted to the confidence of the knowing; they are then often fondled, and make slaves of their admirers for the secrets extracted from them. So it is that, within the memory of men, new sciences are forming, and are accepted, from what were con-

sidered at one time but dreams and ridiculous
speculations. But, if we suffer, we grow wise
with time. There are notably among the dis-
coveries, we may say of the present age, such
representative words as Anthropology, Ethnology, and Philology—kindred sciences, each of
which, while possessing great interest for the
ordinary reader, makes it compulsory upon those
who lay claim to superior education to be at
least acquainted with them. From the mines
of wealth worked by the lovers of these sciences
is collected much that is contained in the following pages. If we shape our own fabric out
of them ; in it will be found nothing to offend
those who follow truth for its own sake, while
respecting the beliefs and prejudices of others.

The subject proposes that the locality of
the Chaldæa of Genesis has not hitherto been
discovered, and that it has not been proven
to have ever existed in the East. Those

who consider it as having been in the East, attach themselves to an error that dates probably from the period of the first migrations of the human family. How? Principally because men, families, and tribes of men—removed in time and place and manifesting their moral and physical nature, through fear, or courage, in defence, offence, spirit of aggrandizement, self-assertion, and from the influences to the *motive* of their existence—seeing in other families and tribes, separated, perhaps from the time of their first dispersion, enemies and encroachers, feel most things but not the truth of their common origin. So to each opposing people the directions taken over the continents, the settlements made, and civil prosperities created by each; or perhaps the kingdoms and civilizations they became aware of, or traded with, or assailed on their way, are for the most part lost to the knowledge of each. What knowledge cannot give, *Idea* supplies; its procession through the mind is grand and imposing according as the cause is great. If great, it has power of inducing awe, and presenting itself in grand assumption, pointing to the *exact* country inhabited by primeval men, the language they spoke, what their religion was, and conjures up everything necessary to the seeming of truth, and the *obligation* of recording events and things! Like stars looking through the majesty of night, the elements of truth sparkle in *Idea*, and give spread and consequence to its creation; and to no ebullition of fancy so much as that which forms around the truth of man's first existence—his locations and wander on earth to another existence.

The fact is, mankind has been long persuaded that in the East was contained almost all the Scripture sites. Wrongly interpreting what we are told in Genesis, that the beginning

of Nimrod's kingdom was "Babel, and Erech,
and Accad, and Calneh *in the land of Shinar,*"
and that Asshur *went out* of that land "and
builded Nineveh," &c., has assisted more than
anything else to make this believed. But,
nevertheless, it has always been a complete
mystery where was Shinar. Mistaking the
situation of Shinar, made it necessary to find
Chaldæa and other countries either *in* or *near* it.
Thus, Shinar is supposed to mean in Hebrew
(as shown in our pages), something like *two-
river.* This signification no doubt was found
because it was thought it must be near or
between the Tigris and Euphrates. But, even
if the etymology be admitted, it is an unsatis-
factory explanation of the position of so important a place as we must believe Shinar
to have been. Shinar, to the Commentators,
is often only a convertible term for Aram-
Naharam, and Mesopotamia, which bear an

interpretation " between the rivers," or the country between the Tigris and Euphrates. As to Chaldæa, the name has no meaning in any of the Semitic tongues.

We refer the earnest inquirer to our text for full information on the state of the question.

CONTENTS.

CHAPTER I.

THE EXTENT OF CHALDÆA—ITS SITUATION NOT
IN THE EAST.

PAGE

Mr. Rawlinson cited 2
Supposed etymologies of Shinar, Chaldæa, . . 5
Aram-Naharaim, Mesopotamia, Al-Jezireh, Babylon 6
New Edition of the Bible referred to . . . 7
Babel, Erech, Accad, Calneh—Calah and Calno not
the same 8
The Celtic Languages—Necessity of acquaintance
with for Proper Study of the Bible . . . 9

CHAPTER II.

REMARKS ON THE SONS OF NOAH AND THEIR
TONGUES.

The First Descendants of the Sons of Noah and
their Locations 11
Arbitrary Classification of Languages . . . 12
The Kratylos of Plato—Plato probably had no idea
of penetrating the Relationship of Languages . 13
Max Müller and the Aryan and Semetic Tongues . 14
The Lingua-Prisca of the first inhabitants of Italy
a Dialect of 'Primitive Celtic 17
Table of Aryan words from Max Müller's Compara-
tive Mythology, imperfect in Celtic examples . 18
"The Principles that must guide the Student of the
Science of Language" not established . . 21
Examples of English, Irish, Chaldee, and Hebrew
Primitive words 22

CHAPTER III.

SHINAR IS EUROPE.

Page

The People of Shem, Ham, and Japhet proposed to
be traced in pre-historic Europe 24
Hebrew and Celtic etymology of the word Shinar . 25
Supposed Eastern Kingdoms, and People to be
found in the *West* and *not* in the East . . 26

CHAPTER IV.

CHALDÆA IS IN WESTERN EUROPE—REFERENCE TO THE RELIGION OF THE CHALDEES.

Remains of the Great Chaldæan Nation can be par-
ticularly distinguished in Great Britain and Ire-
land 28
The words Calneh and Chaldæa 29
Examples of Names of Places and People in Great
Britain to which the word *Cal* is prefixed . . 30
Accad—Many names of Ecclesiastical Foundations
in Ireland, compounded of this word . . . 30
Orcad, Ocad 31
Similarity of Celtic and Arabic tradition . . 32
The Saxon " Genesis " 33
b'Raschith 33
b'Cadmin 33
What was Druidism ? 34
The Chasidim, or Assidæan, names of People of
Chaldæa—perhaps the same as the Essenian,
afterwards represented by the Culdees . . . 35
Pythagoras taught much of his Philosophy by the
Druid Abaris 36
Cause of the Greeks knowing little of the Gæls . 37

CHAPTER V.

UR OF THE CHALDEES—REFERENCE TO IRELAND AS UR.

PAGE

Eber and Heber 39
The Irish Heber, a Hebrew 40
Heber welcomed in Ireland by Druids and ladies of
    the race, and name of Lughaid or Lud, the
    brother of Arphaxad 42
Name of the Descendants of Lud in the British Isles 42
The Irish Round Towers. 44
Aryan and Semetic names of Irish Saints . . 48
Much of the Ancient Literature of Ireland destroyed
    by the Early Christians 49
Intercourse between the East and Ireland . . 49
Stone Remains in Ireland that must have originated
    with the People of Genesis 50

CHAPTER VI.

THE CROSS OF CHALDÆAN SYMBOL . . . 53

CHAPTER VII.

THE SONS OF NOAH AND THEIR DESCENDANTS.

The Welsh believe Hu the Mighty to have been the
    same as Noah and Xisuthrus 56
The Irish and the Hebrews trace their Genealogies
    up to Noah 57
The name Hu, in its modifications, peculiar to
    Wales, Ireland, and England 57
SECTION I.
The Seven Sons of Japhet 58

Contents.

PAGE

Ancient Greek and Roman writers agree that the
Celts, or Cymry, or Gomeridæ were the primo-
genital family 60
Cymbri, or Humbri, or Umbri of Italy . . . 61
The Welsh pride themselves upon being sons of
Gomer 62
Magog, Javan, Ashkenez, Rippath 62
Togamah, Elisah, Tarshish 63
Dodanam, Dedanim, Tuath-de-Danaan . . . 64

CHAPTER VIII.

THE SONS OF HAM, AND HIS DESCENDANTS IN WESTERN EUROPE—PROPHESY AGAINST THE "ISLES," AND RETROSPECT OF HABAKUK.

Ham, Hammonah, Hammon Gog 66
English names to which Ham is prefixed . . 67
Cain, Kean, Keane, Kane, Kaine, Kain, Du Cane,
Cann, etc. 68
Cush, Cushandal, Cushenden 68
Midian, Madian, Meath, Midhe, etc. . . . 68
The words of Habakkuk 69
Disturbed Geological Formation in Ireland . . 70
"Eruption of Lakes" 71
A Description of "Bogs and Ancient Forests" . 72
Iolo MSS. quoted 74
The Psalms, as well as the Books of the Prophets,
allude to a great convulsion 78
The Koran and the Inhabitants of the Wood near
Median—Midianite Merchantmen . . . 78
Ninevite Sculptures and Remains at Cashel . . 79
Egyptian, Indian, and Arab monuments have their
Celtic art affinities 80

CHAPTER IX.

CUSH AND NIMROD.

PAGE

Semiramis and Ninus, Belus, Babylon, Bel . . 81
Rhea or Cybele originated from Semiramis . . 82
Kronos, or Saturn, was not only Cush, Bel or Bal,
but Ninus or Nimrod ; Nimrod (Kronos) King of
the Cyclops, who were his brethren, and the inventors of Tower-building 83

CHAPTER X.

CUTHITES AND HYPERBOREANS.

Hyperboreans, erroneously called Cuthites, extend
their Settlements to Asia, and southward to Africa 85
Hyperboreans, called Scindi, and Sauromatæ, and
Arimaspians 86
Apollo retired to their Country. 87
Iran and Irin, Erin 87
Hyperborean Rites said to have been brought to
Delos 88
The Mons Palatinus and the Hyperboreans . . 88
Hyperboreans looked upon themselves as of the
same Family as the Gods 89
Ireland, the Home of the Hyperboreans . . . 90
The word Hyperborean 90
Iberians originally Hebrew 94

CHAPTER XI.

THE SONS OF SHEM.

Traces of the Sons of Shem numerous in Europe . 95
The Pastoral Staff, the Winged Bull, the Winged
Lion ; Asshurbani-pal ; Arphaxad . . . 96

PAGE

Prydian, the origin of the name Britain . . . 97
The Serpent, a Chaldæan and Israelitish sign . 97
The Serpent, a Mysterious Sign 98
Carnac in Brittany 100
Pight, Picti, Pict, derived from *Phaxad* . . . 101
St. Patrick and Serpent Worship 102
Lud, Arphaxad, and Aram 102
The Game of Troy in Wales 103
What Josephus says of Uz, Ul, and Gether, &c. . 104

CHAPTER XII.

SALA.

Cær-Salug 105
Ban-Chors 105
Cær-Evrog, Eboricum, the old name of York . . 106
Levi and Lewis 106
Freemasonry and the Chaldæan Mysteries . . 108
The Cornish contains Hebrew 109
William the Conqueror and the House of Israel . 110
The Psalter of " Old Sarum " 111
" Salah," in the Psalms 112
The Mahometan Story of Salah, &c. . . . 112
Names of places prefixed by the word *Sala* . . 112
Names of people prefixed by the name . . . 113

CHAPTER XIII.

HEBER.

Heber, the Crowned-Horseman 114
In the days of Heber, Jocktan, and Peleg, a
    division of the Earth 115
Jocktan takes a Tribe into Arabia 115
A few Arab and Celtic Traditions 115

Contents.   xxiii

PAGE

Hud as a Prefix to names in England . . . 121
Peleg and Pelasgus 122
The Tower of Babel and the Hebrew Language . 123
DESCENDANTS FROM HEBER 124

CHAPTER XIV.

TERAH AND ABRAM.

Thamud and Thomond 125
Tera and Tara—Teman, Teman's town, Midian,
   and Cushan 126
Tailten and Teltown 126
Temhair-na-Riogh 127
Cormac's Palace at Tara 127
Other buildings at Tara 130
Poets who have written of Ancient Tara—Keneth
   O'Hartigan 131
Excerpt from his poem 132
Ireland, and Terah and Abram 136
The *Thera*puetes and Essenes 138
The Tardala and Tarleise of Spain, people of
   Abram 138
Abram and Sarai 139
Rebekah and Eleazar 142
Rebekah and Isaac 145
JACOB AND ESAU 147
A verse in the Book of Ballymote 151
Edom, Red Earth, Man, Adam 151
Moab 151
The Situation of Teman entirely unsuspected by
   Writers on Bible History 153
Flocks and Herds, Speckled and Spotted Cattle, &c. 155
Hazel and Green Poplar, not Eastern Trees . . 155

PAGE

Mr. Rawlinson and the Mineral Resources and
Climate of the supposed Neighbourhood of Ur   157
Sir Robert Kane and the "Industrial Resources of
Ireland   159
Gerard Bote and the Brooks and Springs of Ire-
land   164
Jacob and his Uncle Laban   165
Most of the Names of Jacob's Children yet found in
the British Islands   167
Gilead in Ireland   168
Jacob sets up a Stone for a Pillar   168
LEGEND OF THE LIA FAIL; OR, STONE OF DES-
TINY   169
Geological Account of the Stone   178
Mahanaim and *Jegar-Sahadutha*   182
ᚷᚪᛚᛚ·ᛚᛠᚷ, and *Galeed*   183
Covenant on Mount Gilead   185
Colony of Edomites Settled in Italy   . . .   187
Sier and Gebal   187
Gabhal and Gael   . .   אֱלוֹף   . . .   188
The Dukes of Edom—אֱלוֹף and Duke   . . .   189
Gebalines—Guelphs and *Guibelines*   191
Edin and *Eden*   192
God *Ees*   193
Gble, Keble, Gabla mean Cabala—"Gblm," "Stone-
Squarers," and "Master-Masons"   . . .   194
Gobban-Saer—Freemason-sage, one of the Guabhres
or Cabiri   194
Aliben. Dysart. *Di-Ees-ard*   195
Dalhraide, the Red Branch of Ulster   . . .   195
CONCLUSION   196

IRELAND,
UR OF THE CHALDEES.

———◆———

CHAPTER I.

THE EXTENT OF CHALDÆA—ITS SITUATION NOT IN THE EAST.

I N bringing before the reader's attention the extent of ancient Chaldæa, (in which was Ur,) according to the best authorities, we do so in order to show that it was of such small dimensions as not to have contained the cities and kingdoms commonly supposed to have been within its area, and therefore that the district or country of Chaldæa was not between the Tigris and Euphrates.

Perhaps the best authority that has appeared lately on this subject is Mr. Rawlinson,* who has been quoted extensively in the notes to the new edition

* The Five Great Monarchies of the Ancient Eastern World,

of the Bible and elsewhere. We give from his work (p. 14) a passage on Chaldæa :— .

" It is obvious. that the only natural divisions of Chaldæa proper are those made by the river courses. The principal tract must always have been that which intervenes between the two streams. This was anciently a district some 300 miles in length, varying from 20 to 100 miles in breadth, and perhaps averaging 50 miles, which must thus have contained an area of about 15,000 square miles. The tract between the Euphrates and Arabia was at all times smaller than this, and in the most flourishing period of Chaldæa must have fallen short of 10,000 square miles.

"We have no evidence that the natural division of Chaldæa here indicated was ever employed in ancient times for political purposes. The division which appears to have been so employed was one into northern and southern Chaldæa, the first extending from Hit to a little below Babylon, the second from Niffer to the shores of the Persian Gulf. In each of these districts we have a sort of tetrarchy, or special pre-eminence of four cities, such as appears to be indicated by the words, ' The beginning of his

kingdom was Babel, and Erech, and Accad, and
Calneh, in the land of Shinar.'* The southern
tetrarchy is composed of the four cities—Ur, or Hur,
Huruk, Nipur, and Larsa, or Larancha, which are
probably identified with the Scriptural 'Ur of the
Chaldees,' Erech, Calneh, and Ellasar.† The northern
consists of Babel or Babylon, Borsippa, Cutha, and
Sippara, of which all, except Borsippa, are mentioned
in Scripture.‡ Besides these cities, the country contained many others, as Chilmad, Dur-kurri-galzu, Ihi,
or Ahava, Rubesi, Duran, Tel-Humba, &c. *It is not
possible at present to locate with accuracy all these places.
We may, however, in the more important instances fix,
either certainly, or with a very high degree of probability, their position.*

* Gen. x. 10. His note is, "The sacred historian, perhaps,
further represents the Assyrians as adopting the Babylonian
number on their emigration to the more northern regions :—' Out
of that land went forth Asshur, and builded Nineveh, and the
city Rehoboth, and Calah, and Resen.' (Gen. x. 11, 12.)"

† "In three out of these four cases the similarity of the name
forms a sufficient ground for the identification. In the fourth
case the chief ground of identification is a statement in the
Talmud that Nopher was the site of the Calneh of Nimrod."

‡ "Sippara is the Scriptural Sepharvaim. The Hebrew term
has a dual ending, because there were two Sipparas, one on
either side of the river."

"Hur or Ur, the most important of the early capitals, was situated on the Euphrates, probably at no great distance from its mouth. It was probably the chief commercial emporium in the early times, as in the bilingual vocabularies its ships are mentioned in connection with those of Ethiopia.* The name is found to have attached to the extensive ruins (now about six miles from the river, on its right bank, and nearly opposite its junction with the Shat-el-Hie) which are known by the name of Mugheir, or 'The Bitumened.'" †

Now the substance of all this is, that Chaldæa proper was divided by the river courses, or, in other words, lay between the Tigris and Euphrates, " anciently a district some 300 miles in length," and " perhaps averaging 50 miles in breadth;" and that the other tract between the Euphrates and Arabia was 10,000 square miles, or less than a third of the entire Chaldea, calculated to have had an extent of 23,000 square miles—falling short of Ireland by

---

* " Sir H. Rawlinson in the *Journal of the Geographical Society*, vol. xxvii., p. 185."

† " Mr. Taylor in the *Journal of the Asiatic Society*, vol. xv., p. 260. Sir H. Rawlinson prefers the derivation of *Um-qir*, ' the mother of bitumen.' "

more than 9000 square miles. Then Mr. Rawlinson, in the wake of those who have written upon the subject before him, goes on to tell us of the *"probable"* situation of Ur or Hur, and that according to Sir H. Rawlinson, it was *"probably"* the chief commercial emporium in the early times. It is not to be wondered at that Mr. Rawlinson follows upon the beaten track of discovery in this quarter —it is far safer so to do than to search for truth in a new direction, which, however, is enticing, and affording abundance to gratify the thinker, the archæologist, and scholar. Handed down to us are etymologies of names of places, doubtful as the positions of those places :

The word Shinar suggests what is given as the Hebrew of it, *nothing more:—*

Shin שְׁנֵי " two," and נָהָר " *nahr*" or " *ar*," a river.

Chaldæa is rendered, אֶרֶץ כַּשְׂדִּים, "the country," or " dry land of Chasdim," which word is no doubt derived from Chased, son of Nahor, who gave his name to the city of Nahor in Aram-Naharaim.

Aram-Naharaim, אֲרָם נַהֲרַיִם, Aram, " between the

rivers." In Syriac, *Beth-Nahrin* has the same signification. The Greeks from the Hebrew, or Syriac, consequently compounded a word with the same meaning—

Mesopotamia (Μεσοποτάμια), or the Country between Rivers.

The Arabs knew it by the name of "The Island," or

Al-Jezireh.

Babylon, in Greek, Βαβυλών, and in Hebrew בבל Babel, from Balal, to *confound*, which word is said to be contracted from *Balbal, confusion.* There are other etymologies, but the latter are the most probable, and have the advantage of signifying exactly the state in which the question is involved at the present time— confounded, and in confusion !

We have given the above examples of ancient names of places, because they are generally understood to mean the same thing, *viz.*, the *country* or *land between rivers*—the one exception seems to be the Arabic *Al-Jezireh*, or "The Island." How these interpretations may be otherwise understood than they are intended, we will afterwards consider. At present it is obvious that our best scholars are undecided as to the correct meaning and geographical position of Shinar, Chaldæa, Aram-Naharaim, Mesopotamia, Al-Jezireh, or even Babylon. We have looked in vain through the notes to the new edition of the Bible, and thought, (as we believe most people would, before risking a conclusion to so important a question,) that the great intellects engaged upon that work would have evolved something tangible from the many hypotheses that have been constructed in defence of *a locality* for these most important Scripture places. The authorities for the new edition of the Bible have simply quoted from the best writers upon the subject. To Mr. Rawlinson they owe a great deal, but he unfortunately has left the question much in the same way as he found it. This is what was to be expected, for all the misapprehension about the question has originated with the interpreters of the Bible making Shinar, Chaldæa, Aram-Naharaim, Mesopotomia, and Babylon one place, and this principally because the words have a like meaning.

Calah is confounded by Rawlinson with *Calneh.* In Gen. x. 10, it is stated that the beginning of Nimrod's kingdom was Babel, Erech, Accad, and Calneh, in the land of Shinar; but in verses 11 and 12 of the same chapter it is given—" Out of *that* land went forth Asshur, and builded Nineveh, and the city Rehoboth, and *Calah*, and Resen, between Nineveh and *Calah*." Beside Calah and Calneh, there is a *Calno* quoted by some authors as the same place. There is nothing very strange in supposing Asshur to have been the builder of Calah. Calah and Calneh were *not* the same place. Calah, it may be allowed, was in the district claimed for it by Rawlinson, but that Calneh was not there, it is sufficient to know—" Asshur went out " of a land called Shinar, of which Calneh, with Babel, Erech, and Accad, was the *beginning*, (Heb. ראשית,* *rashith*). Asshur is described as having gone out of Shinar, and built the cities of Nineveh, Rehoboth, Resen, and *Calah*. For the situations of these cities there is ample evidence. The *beginning* of the kingdom of Nimrod should be understood as distinct from the building of Nineveh, Calah, and other cities in Assyria, attributed to Asshur.

Interpreters of Scripture, misled by often only a *supposed* meaning of the Bible names of places which

---

* So probably the Al-Rass of the Khoran means simply, " the beginning."

they find in Chaldee, Hebrew, and Greek, and misled also by their anxiety to find all the beginnings of things in the East, have mistaken the testimony of the aboriginal language of Europe, and the countries over which it was spoken—that language admitted by philologists to have been before Greek and Latin, and co-existing with Sanskrit; the language that gave names' to most of the mountains, rivers, the natural scenery of Europe, and bestowed on parts of Asia cognate words that endure yet almost unchanged— . the Celtic. If those interpreters had availed themselves of the light shed by the Celtic languages upon the pages of the Bible over which they laboured, they would not have sanctioned the huddling together of so many countries and cities in Chaldæa—a place not to be found even in name in the whole Hebrew Bible.*

If it is our duty to seek the best means of proof, it is necessary to divest ourselves of prejudice while thinking over the " Book" that contains so many truths about our first state and our future life.

---

* As before stated Chaldæa is rendered אֶרֶץ כַּשְׂדִּים (Arts-Chasdim), the country, or dry land of Chasdim.

CHAPTER II.

REMARKS ON THE SONS OF NOAH AND THEIR TONGUES.

WHERE the habitation of Noah was after his descent of Ararat, has not yet been discovered, at any rate, satisfactorily; but we are informed it was a land in which "he planted a vineyard," according with him being a husbandman. His sons, after living with him for a time in this unascertained locality—as unascertained as the eastern resting-place of the Ark— separated. Of the descendants of Japhet, the elder son, we are told they occupied the immense extent of land that stretches from Asia Minor, immediately south of the Caspian sea, the river Oxus, the Iamus and Attay Mountains, to the extreme east and north of Asia,* and westward over Asiatic and European Scythia, Scandinavia, Britain, Gaul, Italy, Greece, all the Mediterranean islands, and into Asia Minor again;

* Why they may have gone over to America from this or some other point, is a matter that does not come within the range of the present argument; although it cannot be treated upon here, it is related to our subject.

by many it is thought the west coast of Asia Minor, or Dodanim, bordering upon *a* Tarshish, which they include, with the island of Cyprus on its south, in the Japhetian chart. Shem's descendants are supposed to have inhabited all the land south of the Iamus and Attay Mountains, to the east and north as far as Japan; southward, over the Pacific Islands, Hindostan, Persia, Syria, Assyria—the country of Aram, and then, with the exception of Dodanim, and the supposed Tarshish, the remainder of Asia Minor. The descendants of Ham are assigned to Arabia and Africa. The names of the sons of the generations of Noah can be traced as having been peculiar to Western Europe before Christ.

"The whole earth was of one language, and of one speech. And it came to pass, as they journeyed *from* the east, that they found a plain in the land of Shinar; and they dwelt there." (Gen. xi. 1, 2.) Of course it must be concluded from this, that the sons of Noah *were* of one language and one speech, and that they dwelt in Shinar, which country was in the *West*, for it is expressly stated *they* journeyed *from* the *East*. In what part of the West, *from* Asia, was Shinar, if it did not extend over all Europe, we will leave to the reader to determine from the facts as they are given in our subsequent pages. For the present we safely assume that the sons of Noah spoke *one* language; what that language was may be a difficult question to answer correctly; but difficulty should not deter us from at least searching for it among parts that once made a whole—made *one* language before it effected others.

Notwithstanding the arbitrary classification of languages—philologists are becoming more aware of this fact—it is quite possible that time and observation will reward the independent searchers after truth, and bring together, through them, so many, at least, elements of *the* matrix tongue spoken by the sons of Noah, and for a time their descendants, as will for ever set at rest in solid foundation the materials of the primitive speech. We are aware of the gravity of such a task, and that it requires volumes to do it justice. If we devote a few suggestive pages to this subject it is because they may be found necessary to the explanation of the text, and of service in discovering a European location of Shinar.

The laws of language and the names of those laws were first discovered by the Greek philosophers and grammarians. Yet, as may be gathered from a passage in the Kratylos of Plato, that acute mind could not do more than suggest that the "Barbarians" lent some of their words to the Greek. The idea of penetrating the relationship of languages probably never entered - the head of Plato. It was reserved for the thinkers of this century to take the first step towards the classification of languages. The stupendous mass of speech used by man is, at this hour, as difficult a task to divide into distinct families as any that can be conceived. The Aryan, Semetic, the Indo-Chinese, the Malayo-Polynesian, the Polysynthetic dialects of America, and other tongues have not at present yielded much towards the philosophy of language; but as far as researches have been conducted the Aryan and the Semetic have contributed most. Under the Aryan are comprised the languages of India, Persia, Armenia, Greece, Italy, the Celtic, and the Sclavonic. The Semetic includes the languages of the Babylonians, the Syrians, the Jews, the Ethiopians, and the Arabs. If we judge of the influence of these two classes of language upon political and literary history, we admit they include the most important of the earth.

But inasmuch as it can only, at present, be conjectured what was the first and natural state of language, so is there much tendency to err dividing it into classes. Thus the Sanskrit and Hebrew, the Celtic and Arabic, are not only to be studied as Aryan and Semetic languages, but as languages that must have reciprocated many of their parts. A hundred years ago this would be considered visionary by scholars accustomed to look up Hebrew, Greek, and Latin glossaries for the radicals of various and dissimilar words. But their labour in that way was unproductive—they accepted as necessarily true what had been taught them, nor believed that there might be much darkness dispelled, and some things important to the elucidation of *language* discovered in the histories of people and nations, in the records of their manners and customs in relation to present manners and customs, their names of places and things remaining in modern languages; the wars of people and nations, their contacts, their associations, peace, admixture of race, their civilization, and by their monuments of civilization in decay. Man in his normal state had a vigorous language, uncircumscribed by rules. Max Müller, alluding to the Aryan and Semetic speech owing their origin to historical concentrations of speech wild and unbounded, says :

" In the eyes of the student of language Sanskrit, Greek, and Latin, Hebrew, Arabic, and Syriac are what a student of natural history would not hesitate to call 'monstra,' unnatural, exceptional formations, which can never disclose to us the real character of language left to itself to follow out its own laws, without let or hindrance. For that purpose a study of the Chinese and the Turanian dialects, a study even of the jargons of Africa, Polynesia, Melanesia, is far more instructive than the most minute analysis of Sanskrit and Hebrew." *

Although the historical concentrations, by. which was formed a wild, unbounded Aryan and Semetic speech—the languages of most parts of Asia and Europe—cannot be written in detail, we may arrive at an almost certain conclusion that such a language became the basis of the Zend, Doric, old Sclavonic, Latin, Gothic, Armenian, Lithuanian, perhaps Sanskrit, for all are varieties of one type, and perhaps no one of them can be considered as the original on which the others altogether formed. Who can say from what words grew and diverged dialects and languages ? It is certain that the Sanskrit even, although approaching

* Stratification of Language, p. 10.

so near to *a* matrix language, has not preserved, in many cases, the primitive and organic forms of words to be found in Greek and Latin. This is held by many scholars. Max Müller gives, as an example, that Εσ-μες cannot be derived from the Sanskrit *smas*, because *smas* has lost the radical *a*, which Greek has preserved, the root being *as*, to be, the termination *mas*, we. In the same way the Greek cannot be called a language from which others were derived, for the Latin language has preserved some forms that are older than Greek. So we find ἐντί or ἐνσί (contracted from ἐσεντι) is preserved by *sunt*. Here Greek has dropped the radical *as* altogether, while Latin, like Sanskrit, has at least preserved the radical *s* in *sunt = santi.*

An older language than either may yet be in existence. Those words that were used to signify the nearest necessity of human existence, such as man, woman, father, mother, brother, sister, sky, soul, air, earth, water, bread, wine, strength, work, house, village, town, writing, gate, tower, king, queen, &c., are words that may be said to contain the history of the world, and as they are nearly alike in sound and meaning in the languages above specified, and

also in the Celtic,* the problem of the radical relationship of all languages may one day be solved, and
the disciples of Raumer, Ascoli, and Ewald, no doubt,
be delighted ; at any rate, brought to a confession
that the Aryan and Semetic speakers have preserved
from the earliest time words that prove, not only the
divergence of speech from one speech, but the divergence of race from one race, and consequently from
one locality. The relationship of the Aryan languages
is evident :—

Eng.	Sanskrit.	Zend.	Greek.	Latin.	Gothic.	Slav.	Irish.
Father,	pitár,	patar,	πατήρ,	pater,	fadar,	...	athair.†
Mother,	mátár,	mátár,	μήτηρ,	mater,	...	mati,	mathair.
Brother,	bhrátar,	bráta,	(φρατήρ),	frater,	bropar,	brat,	brathair.
Sister,	svásar,	khanha,	...	soror,	svistar,	sestra,	siur.
Daughter,	duhitar,	dughdhar,	θυγάτηρ,	...	dauhtar(Lith.)	dukte,	dear.

The above, from Max Müller, are only a few of
the words used by the first of the Aryan stock. The
Lingua-Prisca of the first inhabitants of Italy was
nothing more than a dialect of the primitive Celtic.
In course of time this dialect received infusions of
Greek, particularly Æolic, through the adventurers
from the Peloponessus. The Greek itself meantime

* Under Celtic will be included, as well as Irish, the Erse of
Scotland, the Welsh, the Manx, Cornish, and Armoric.

† *Ab*, the same as the Hebrew, is sometimes used for Father
as *Am* is for Mother.

retained much of the ancient Celtic, upon which it undoubtedly grew, as from one extensive root that spread itself everywhere over Europe. We make these remarks in order to point out that the Aryan languages, so called, are in all probability ramifications of the original speech of Europe; and, even if it were only possible that this is the case, the educated should turn their attention to the Celtic language, and, while *knowing*, either prove or disprove the claims put in for its antiquity.

We again turn to Max Müller, who interests us in the old household of the Aryans. That their words tell the story of their pastoral life being a life of peace the following table, principally taken from his Comparative Mythology,* will sufficiently show. It is given because of the great authority of Max Müller; at the same time it is to be regretted that he had not a better acquaintance with the Celtic language, examples of words from which he gives in the paradigm, while other examples ready to his hand, and the equivalents of the very words he introduces for illustration, are left out. We have taken the liberty to insert them.

* Oxford Essays, 1856, p. 26.

	Sanskrit.	Zend.	Greek.	Italian.	Teutonic.	Lithuan.	Slav.	Celtic.
Cattle:	paśu	paśu	πῶυ	pecu	G. faihu	PRUSS. pecku	SLAV. govjado	...
Ox and Cow:	go (nom. gaus)	gâo	βοῦς	bos	O.H.G. fihu	LETT. gohw		I. bo
Ox:	ukshan	ukhshan, vakhsha	...	vacca ?	O.H.G. chuo, G. auhsan	...	...	W. ych
Steer:	sthûrâ	stavra	ταῦρος	taurus	stiur	...	tour	I. tarbh
Heifer:	stari	...	στεῖρα	(sterilis)	stairo	...	...	...
Horse:	âśu, aśva	aspa	ἵππος	equus	G. aihus	aszwa	...	W. osw
Foal:	...	...	πῶλος	pullus	G. fula	...	...	...
Dog:	śvan	spâ (σπāκα)	κύων	canis	O.H.G. hund	szu	R. sobaka, BULG. kuce	G. cu
Sheep:	avi	...	ὄις	ovis	G. avi-str, E. ewe	awi	SLAV. ovja	I. aodh
Calf:	vatsa	...	ἴταλος	vitulus	...	...	...	...
He-goat:	aǵâ	...	κάπρος	caper	O.H.G. hafr	ozis	...	I. gabhar
She-goat:	...	...	αἴξ	...	...	...	...	G. aighe
Sow:	su (kara)	...	ὗς	sus	O.H.G. sû	...	svinia	...
Pig:	prishat	...	πόρκος	porcus	O.H.G. farah	parszas	POL. prosie	I. porc
Hog:	gŕishvi	...	χοῖρος	...	O.N. gris	...	...	...
Donkey:	...	...	ὄνος	asinus	asilo	...	...	I. asal
Mouse:	mûsh	...	μῦς	mus	O.H.G. mûs	musse	POL. mysz	I. luch
Fly:	makshikâ	...	μυῖα	musca	O.H.G. micco	...	R. mucha	...
Goose:	hansa	...	χήν	anser	O.H.S. kans	zasis	BOH. hus	I. geadh

The last word in the list, *goose*, was rendered by Max Müller *"ganra,"* signed by him " *Gaelic*," but it should have been, as now inserted, *géadh*, the same as the Irish for goose. The only difference is that Max Müller makes a goose a gander;—in Saxon, Gaelic, and Irish, and other cognate tongues, *ganra* is gander. The table of words is, however, very valuable as a contribution towards the proof of a primitive oneness of the Aryan languages and people. And if the Semetic glossaries are carefully examined, it will be found that there is not such an estrangement between them and the Aryan as is commonly supposed.

We give a few examples of words from the Chaldaic, Hebrew, and Irish.

They, we hope, will be found sufficient to interest while explaining that these languages must have been radically the same ; those who, having read through the list, would still doubt this, are respectfully asked to reconsider the question, divesting themselves as much as possible of preconception and the influences upon correct judgment that come of school. Let them remember that the *principles* of language are not universally accepted. Nor is this to be wondered at when we come to perceive that man of his vanity

would systematise Tongues, hundreds of which are
not even in their alphabets understood by him. To
the Hebraist, but slightly acquainted with the Celtic
archæology and tongues, we can promise, if he gives
adequate attention to them, that he will be relieved
from much of the idle nonsense diffused by most
philologists and grammarians. We find Max Müller
(in the preface to his " Chips from a German Work-
shop," p. 19) telling us that " the principles that must
guide the student of the science of language "*are now
firmly established.*" We wonder what those *principles*
are, for Max Müller has not discovered them to us,
nor to, as far as we know, any of the numerous
learned societies with which he is connected. Perhaps what he means by *the principles* that must guide
the student of the science of language, is the exercise
of a student's own good judgment, above being
reduced by the awe so often created in his breast
while contemplating the stupendous learning—the
contents of *all* lexicons, all *words disposed* by
grammar and registered on mind—required to unbury
and bring into light, out of the infinitude of speech,
its first laws and elements—there is much work left
for the ambitious !

English.	Irish.	Chaldee.	Hebrew.
Father,	Ab, aba,	אבא aba,	אב ab. The same in Arabic.
Mother,	Am, (so Mam, as in Welsh)	אם am,	אם am.
Huzza !	Abou !*	אבוי aboui,	אבוי aboui.
Son,	Orc,†	יך irc,	יך irc, irac.
A gale, a wind, a blast,	Atha,	עתי ati.	... The same in Arabic.
Attic (old),	Atac,	עתק atac.	עתיק athic.
A child,	Bab, baban,	(באבן) babun ; Phœnician.)	Arabic, babus.
A sage, a prophet,	Baid,	בדא bada ; Sanskrit, budda, wise.	
A currant or sacred cake,	Bairin-Breac, the speckled or sacred cake,‡	ברק barac.	Arabic, barakut.
The Lord, the sun,	Bal, or Beal,	בעל baal, bal.	בעל baal.
White,	Ban,	לבן laban, to whiten, from the root ban.	
Son or youth,	Bar,	בר bar ; Persian, 'beirma, youth.§	

* War cry, as "O'Domnhall Abou !"   † Literally means the inside of the thigh ; generally son of a prince.
‡ Offered to the moon, or queen of heaven, at the autumnal equinox, now St. Michael's day, 29th September.
§ Probably bairn, used in Scotland for child, is so derived.

English.	Irish.	Chaldee.	Hebrew.
Mouth,	Cab (corrupt, gob),	קב *kab.*	
Holy, sacred,	Cad,	—	קדש *kadas*, a sanctuary, from the Irish root *cad.*
Miserable, poor,	Dall,	דל *dal.*	
A servant,	Lac,	לאך *lak*; from *lac* the word *lackey* is derived.	
Morning,	Maiddin,	מדינה *medinah*; *matin* is probably from *maiddin.*	
Mirth,	Meis,	מחיז *mehiz.*	
Guardian angels, fairies,	Meisi,	מעזי *mezi.*	עז *az*, strength.
Custom,	Nos,	נשא *nesa*, experience.	
Ode,	Odh, music,	—	Arabic, *ada*, Spanish, *laud, alaud.*
Verse, stanza,	Rann,	רנן *ranna.*	Arabic, *rann.*
A story, news,	Sgel,	סיגל *sigel.*	
A moat, village,	Tuim, toom,	טום *toum.*	
Study, learning,	Ugh,	הגה *haga.*	Probably from the Irish *Ugh-der* is derived the word *Author*, which means the same thing.

24

CHAPTER III.

SHINAR IS EUROPE.

THE way being now, to our mind, clear of the principal objections urged in support of a radical difference between the Aryan and Semetic languages, it becomes our task to show how the people of Shem, Ham, and Japhet, may be traced in pre-historic Europe, and to point out that Shinar is ascertainable to have been Europe, and Chaldæa, with Ur, in its western quarter.

As before stated, Shinar, according to Scripture interpreters, is the country round about Babylon, the great plain, or alluvial country, watered by the Tigris and Euphrates. Shinar *round about Babylon* is as un-meaning as the presumed Hebrew etymology of the name, " *Two-river*,"* and has no reference to the *land* it is supposed to signify. It is slightly different when we interpret Arts-Chasdim (the name *for* Chaldæa), as

* See p. 5.

the *country* or *dry land* of Chasdim. Nearly the same may be said of Aram-Naharam, (which we are told means Aram *between the rivers*), and also of Mesopotamia. As to the meaning of Chaldæa we are left entirely in the dark, neither Chaldee nor Hebrew lexicon, nor the learning and ingenuity of men,* have thrown satisfactory light upon it. He would be an unusually bold spirit who would venture to settle the problem, that because Shinar, Chaldæa, Aram-Naharam, Mesopotamia, have a like meaning, therefore they are all one place in the East. A Celtic etymology for Shinar, would be as near, perhaps nearer, the truth. For instance, Shinar might mean in Irish, *a tract of an old country*, from *sean*, old, and *ar* (*ara*), a tract of country. This is not altogether an etymological venture to suit the present purpose; proper consideration of the old European, Irish, British, and other Celtic remains will, at least, make us reject the explanation of the word through the Hebrew.

Elam and Assur are, no doubt, in that part of Asia

---

* Perhaps we strain to a conclusion in this respect, for its meaning, in Irish (*Ceile de*), is, a *preserver of fires*—a Culdee, from Cal, Cail, Ceill, to burn. Some give the meaning of *Ceill*, as *servant*,—*Gil* (the modern form *Gillie*) is more likely to bear this signification.

now called Mesopotamia. The descendants of Nergal
or Nimrod, with their distinctive Cuthite marks, are
there; but the sons of Shem—Arphaxad, Shelah,
Eber, Peleg, Nahor, Terah; and the sons of Ham—
Cush, Canaan, and Dedan, are to be found with the
Japhetians, *i.e.*, Gomerians, Magogians, Ashkenazians,
Riphatians, and the Elishanian (the Elischan) people,
and those of Tarshish; and to have left particular
traces of themselves in Great Britain and Ireland, in
Armorica and other parts of France, and in Spain;
indeed, throughout Europe, more—far more—than are
to be found in Asia; therefore Shinar, we must claim
to be nothing less than Europe. The reader who
follows us will, it is hoped, be assisted to decide
in favour of the old Celtic Europe, which may be
described as one gigantic archaic deposit, in which
antiquarians, ethnologists, and philologists are quarry-
ing with the most hopeful results.

The peoples and kingdoms referred to in the Bible,
and supposed by commentators to be in the East, are
actually to be found in the *West;* they are *not* to be
found in the East. It shall be our effort to show that,
not only the Celtic tongues and literatures, but the
histories of distinct nations, point all in the one

direction, and that the materials of modern science are daily contributing to the proof of pre-historic Europe being the seat of many places and people mentioned in Holy Writ. We will strive to remove the anomaly, that because there is a small district in Asia, less than Ireland by 9,000 square miles, nearly surrounded by two rivers, that therefore Shinar, Chaldæa, Aram-Naharam, Babylon, Mesopotamia, and a host of other important places *must* have been there.

We will bring to bear more direct evidence in support of our position, which we hope our readers will remember is, Shinar being Europe, could not possibly be situated "round about" a Babylon that was neither an island, nor a part of one, in the East.

CHAPTER IV.

THE first Chaldæan was Arphaxad. The religion
of the early Chaldæan shepherds must have been
that of Noah and his sons. The Chaldæan religion,
so called, must have effected the Hebrew. Up to
the time, as well as after, the sons of Noah became
Chaldæan and, Hebrew, megalithic altars, and sacrifice by fire and prayer, were signs of faith.

The remains of the great Chaldæan nation, can be
particularly distinguished in Great Britain and Ireland,
and these remains have special reference to the
religion of the Chaldæan and the Hebrew. The signification of the word Calneh, which was a place, the
same as Calno, of Chaldæa, will assist to illustrate this.

The first part of the word Calneh, *Cal*, is sometimes varied into *cail*, *gal*, and *ceill*, each of which mean
in Irish, "*to burn*"—it has no meaning in Hebrew
more significant of *fire*. . Sometimes by metonomy,
the same word means "a stone altar," which is

sufficiently indicative of sacrifice by "fire and smoke." Now, on the position we would establish as to the affinity of the Semetic and Aryan languages, the Hebrew nearly representing the one, as the Celtic may be said to almost represent the other; and *because* of their affinity, we will look into the Hebrew for the other portion of the word Cal*neh*, and accordingly we discover that *nah*, or *neh* (נאה) as in Jer. xxiii. 10, means a "*pleasant habitation*," or "*a house*," as in Jer. ix. 10; xxv. 37; and in Ps. lxxxiii. 12. So the word Calneh may be taken to signify the *house, e.g.*, *people*, who sacrifice by *fire*. Or according to Gesenius, the *neh* (or *nai*, נה) may come of Arabic, and mean "to shine," as denoting "excellence," "greatness," "beauty." To say the word means *to shine*, is not so figurative as what may be understood from the three words following it, for the reason that it nearly expresses the principal quality of *cal*, or fire, that is, *to burn*.

Calneh, probably was the origin of the word Chaldæa. If we take it apart from *Arts-Chasdim*, its name in Hebrew, we have only to account for the affix *dæa* and it becomes intelligible. Then if *dæa* be interpreted as the beneficent דיא, or God, of the Irish, and not the δαι-μων, generally under-

stood,* we will avoid much of the ridiculous uncertainty presented to us in the rendering of the word
through the Hebrew; for instance, Chaldæa is given
by Calmet: " As dæmons, or as robbers, or breasts, or
fields, from שֵׁד shed, שָׁדֵד shaded, or שָׂדֶה shadah,
and כִּי *ki.*" There is no doubt of the word having its
proper meaning in the Irish, for ᴅᴊᴀ is God in that
language, so *Cal* and *dæa* mean the *fire or altar of
the God.*

The word Calneh is still preserved in the present
English as the name of a borough market town and
parish—Calne, in Wiltshire. We find that *Cal* is
prefixed to many other names of places and families,
such as Caldar, North, South, East, and West, Calder,
or *Cawder*, the Calder Stones near Liverpool, Calder
Bridge, Calder Abbey, Cumberland, and the river
known by that name in the same place. It is also
found in the word Kirk*cal*dy, which •may originally
have meant a place of the *Church* of the *Culdee.*

Beside Calneh we have Accad. The Accad of
Genesis x. 10 is another of the beginnings of Nimrod's
kingdom. That there are many places called Accadh

---

* Δαιμων or spirit. The "Dæmon" of Socrates was a divine
sign, a prophetic and supernatural voice.

on this side of Europe we see at once by referring to the topography of Ireland, where there are numerous names of ecclesiastical foundations compounded of this word :—Achade-Dagain (St. Dagan), in Waterford ; Achad-Ur (Freshford), Kilkenny ; Acad-Garbain, another name for Dungoon, Waterford ; Achadh-Chaoin (the Gentle Achad), another name for Achonry, Sligo ; besides many others.* The word is used more extensively in Ireland if we take it in its corrupted form of Aghar (Lat. *ager*), a field. Agherdruim is rendered *the field of the Druid.*

The Orcads, or Orkneys, as they are now spelt, is another example of the word, which seems to point, however strange it may appear, to the *Ocad*, or Fair of the Arabs, the "holy gathering for the singing of golden verses." We have in *Ocad*, as in *Accad*, the word *cad*, which means in Celtic, in Hebrew,† and Arabic, *holy*. The *Accad* of Genesis no doubt refers to an *Accad* that *is to be found*, not to an *Accad* that has puzzled scholars determined to make an

---

* See Keane's Temples and Towers of Ireland, p. 87.

† קדוש, *Kadosh*, the Hebrew of the present day would say for "holy ! holy ! holy !" "kadosh ! kadosh ! kadosh !" The Arabs say, for the same thing, "kaddus ! kaddus ! kaddus !" *Al-kadr* is the most holy night of the Koran.

eastern *locus* for it. And where should we look
for *Accad,* but to the place that gives us so many
examples of the name. Because Jocktan leading
the Arabs over Europe was contemporaʌy with a Celtic-
speaking people, and there was not time for Arabic to
have taken the form of a distinct language, so the
Arabs preserved many Celtic significations, and many
legends, customs, and religious rites. What is called
Arab tradition is often corroborative of Celtic tradition, as well as Old Testament history.

Cader-Idris to the Arab signifies *the holy place of
Enoch;* strange this should be the name of a mountain
in the principality of Wales !

The Arab history of "Ad and Thamud, Hud, Sala,
those who dwelt at Al-Ras," and " the inhabitants of
the wood near Midian," is singularly enough drawn
from traditions preserved in the verses of the Ocads,
bearing an almost perfect resemblance to the Triads
of the Druids. The *Ocads,* or " *holy fields,*" suggest
the idea of religious teaching. The Accad of
Genesis is not only one of the *beginnings* of Nimrod's kingdom, for from it, as an institution, arose
the *Acadahs* of Ireland, the Ocads of Arabia, the
Academies of Greece. How near this bears upon the

Cadmus who is said to have introduced letters into Greece is better seen when we consider that the Phœnician alphabet had, like the old Irish, but sixteen letters.

The Saxon " *Genesis,*" generally supposed to have been written by a Cædmon, should, we are inclined to think, be understood as simply the *beginning.* This will appear when it is remembered that Cædmon is the initial word of the book of Genesis in the Chaldee paraphrase or Targum of Onkelos, בקדמין b'Cadmin, or b'Cadmon (the *b* is merely prefixed), which is a literal translation of b'Raschith ("*In principio*"), the initial word of the original Hebrew text. It may be hardly necessary to observe that the Jews quote and call the first book of the Bible "b'Raschith"—the books are denominated according to their initial letters. The Chaldaic Genesis, even to the present day, is quoted and called by the Jews *b'Cadmin.*

קדמין, as an adjective, may be translated *eastern*, as it is from the root קדם, *Kedem, the east.* A secondary meaning some of the words derived from this root have when they signify *beginning*, or *commencement*, as much as to express that light, the sun, and day come from the *east.*

D

The religion of Great Britain and Ireland was Druidism. And what was Druidism?—The worship of one God by sacrifice on unhewn stone altars, after the custom of Noah (Gen. viii. 20, 21, 22). The Druids preserved the religion of Noah. There were three orders of the Druids; they were called by their people *Eachdrædth*, which word is yet in the Celtic dialect; the *drædth* being pronounced nearly the same as Druid. The Ur-Bruides of the Irish, as may be gathered from Nennius and others, were the same as the Druids and Bards of the Welsh. The three orders were:—the High Priest, or Chief Druid, who wore white; the *Bard*, blue; the *Ovate*, green. Green was the holy colour of the Ócad of the Arabs, and was carried by them in remembrance of Al-Ras and Irem, the country, according to the Koran, from which they came. The Bancors, or stone circles, were the places where the white priests assembled for sacrifice and song. The word Bancor is made up of the Irish **bꞁaꞃ**, *white*, and **coꞁꞁꞇ**, *cora*, a choir. So *ban* is understood in the word Al*bion*, signifying the land of the white cliffs, the ancient Britain. Ireland had a name with a similar meaning—Banba. The white mantles of the shepherd kings, who were priests, have been always held as signs of purity; hence the modern priests and the choristers are arrayed in white. The Chasidim, or Assidæan, חסידים, 'Aσαδαῖοι—other names for the people of Chaldæa—have given us a clue to the Essenians, no doubt the same as the Assidæans, who, it will be shown, were afterwards represented by the Culdees. The Essenians are given as *Asdanim* in Macc. vii. 13. Josephus, Philo, Pliny, and others, commend the manner of living of the Essenians. After their captivity, the members of the Jewish Church divided into the Chasidim, who superadded the constitutions and traditions of their elders, and the *Zadikim*, or righteous, who observed only the written law of Moses.

"The Chasidim were the Chassidæans or Assidæans. The Hebrew *heth* (the *ch* in English) is expressed in Greek sometimes by an aspirate, in Latin by an *h*, or it may be that it is sometimes entirely omitted as in Assidæans." *—Prid.*, Connect., &c., Part II., bk. iii.

Let us now turn our attention to the Erech or Arach, ארך (in Greek 'Ορέχ, or 'Αρὲκ). It is said

---

* Tal-Iesin, a name frequently applied to Welsh bards, is explained as the head of the Essenians, from Tal the head or leader of the Essenians—so the word *tall* is preserved in English.

to mean, *length*, or what *lengthens*, otherwise *health*, *physic*, from אורכה, Arecah. The supposed eastern city of Erech, Ptolemy places, under the name Aracca, near where the Tigris and Euphrates meet in Susiana. If the word is considered in connection with the *Arecha* of Ammianus—the place of the Arectæan fields, abounding in naphtha, and as a consequence subject to take fire, we then refer its meaning to the first part of *Ar*ach, or *Er*ech, substituting for *er* the Hebrew *Ur* or *Ar, fire* or *light*. What are we forced to draw from this?—simply that *Ur* in Irish (as well as cal) signifies that which burns (ᴜᴩ, fire). That the Hebrew and Irish languages reciprocate many of their words is as true as that the people who once spoke Hebrew had a common origin with those called Celts—first by the Greeks who were nearly innocent of who the *Gcadhals*, or *Gæls*, were, and of their country, even in the time of Pythagoras who nevertheless has acknowledged he was taught much of his philosophy by one of their country, the Druid Abaris. This fact has had the advantage of special authentication, and, if we are to see anything in it, it is that there was a high state of civilization and learning in the land of Abaris, while the philosophy and learning of

Greece was as yet unsystematised, and its people only striving to know how to perpetuate their glory. The *Gæl* had one disadvantage, in directly establishing in the minds of the Greeks the knowledge of his learning and civil greatness, and that was, that his country was distant, and without, as far as we judge, a rival nation to dispute its dominancy in the west, whereas the growing ambition of Rome, situated near to Greece in her zenith, acted for a time to encourage her military and aggrandizing efforts until at last Greece was to an extent absorbed — but meantime, the Romans received the refining influence of her learning and arts, and assisted, more than can be correctly estimated, to spread the knowledge of her greatness, as their arms extended throughout the west of Europe. After a time Christianity made its way; and the learning of the Fathers, having had to operate more or less upon the pagan beliefs of Greece and Rome, while doing so, necessarily handed down to the modern Biblicast and Classicist the full growth of Greek and Roman insight and teaching, which of course included the little known of their origin.

It never, as we have said before, entered the minds

of the Greeks—nor did it enter the Roman mind—
that the elements of their languages, as well as of
their blood, might be proved to have originated with a
people in whose land are monuments as wonderful
and as old as the Cyclopian structures of Greece and
Rome, and whose religion, full of beauty, mystery,
and philosophy, lingers yet in the mind and heart,
not only of the Hebrew and the Catholic, but the
Mahometan and the modern Greek.

It will not require much to convince the impartial
investigator that, if Ur has the same meaning 'in
Irish as in Hebrew, the word, as it was applied,
must in some way be attached to whatever commemo-
rates the old Faith—we use it purposely in the
singular—of those people. And as our means of
proving them as having been identical is forthcoming,
we will, for the present, turn from Erech to the place
that has bewildered antiquarians and scholars in their
search for it—we mean Ur—Ur of the Chaldees.

CHAPTER V.

UR OF THE CHALDEES—REFERENCE TO IRELAND

AS UR.

HAVING, we consider, fully introduced the question that Chaldæa was in the west of Europe,
(although we have only given our reasons, in part, for
so placing it,) it becomes necessary to refer here, in
connection with Ur, to an Old Bible personage of
importance—the grandson of Arphaxad—Eber, or
Heber.

There is found in Irish tradition a Heber whose
name was given to Ireland, and which is to be per-
ceived in the word *Hiber*nia. Whether the Bible
Heber and the Heber of Irish history may be the
same, does not concern us so much as the fact, that
Ireland has preserved to the present time more distinct marks of the ancient Ur than can be pointed to
in any other country, whether of Asia or Europe.

Besides Ireland having had once the name of
Hibernia, from Heber, there are names derived of
Heber in England and Scotland ; in Scotland, the

Hebrides ; in England, the old name of York, Eboricum or Hebericum.

It may appear, as the argument unfolds itself, that the balance of proof will rest on the side of the Irish Heber having been a veritable *Hebr*ew. A stronghold of the Hebrew was *Iberia*, a name under which Spain was once known. A great deal of the mystery that surrounds Heber may be cleared away when we remember our teaching, that the Scripture Hebrew was Chaldæan first, and then Hebrew,* and afterwards Israelite; and that it is recorded that Milesius, the father of the Heber of Ireland, came with his son out of Iberia into Ireland. Iberia and Tarshish are acknowledged by most of our recent Bible commen- tators to be *one place*, that is Spain.

It is told us in Ps. lxxii. 10, in the prayer of David for his son Solomon, that "The kings of Tarshish and of the isles shall bring presents;" there is good testimony in this of the prosperity of Iberia.

---

* "And there came one that had escaped, and told Abram the *Hebrew ;* for he dwelt in the plain of Mamre the Amorite, brother of Eshcol, and brother of Aner ; and these *were* confederate with Abram" (Gen. xiv. 13). This seems the first mention of "Hebrew ;" but there is a Hebron, a place, referred to in Gen. xiii. 18.

We think the position of Tarshish *out of* the East brings many other supposed eastern places with it westward. The allusion to the kings of the isles of the sea carries also significance, probably meaning the British Isles. The remains of the old Heberian Spain, may be said to be present in the designation *Celtiberia*, and no doubt *Gallacia*. Whether we can reconcile the two Hebers to have been one and the same person, is, as we have said before, of little consequence in considering Ur of the Chaldees, Ireland.

The first mention made of Ur is in Gen. xi. 28 :— "And Haran died before his father Terah in the land of his nativity, in Ur of the Chaldees." The next reference is in the 31st verse of the same chapter, as follows :—"And Terah took Abram his son, and Lot the son of Haran his son's son, and Sarai his daughter-in-law, his son Abram's wife; and they went forth with them from Ur of the Chaldees, to go into the land of Canaan ; and they came unto Haran, and dwelt there." It is to be understood, that we interpret the foregoing passages as meaning that Terah belonged to Ur as we place it, and went eastward to Canaan. The district called Haran, no doubt, received its name through Terah, in remembrance of his son Haran, who died in *Ur*. It is possible that there was a county, or district, of Haran in Ireland at the time of Terah's departure, or subsequently, for there are names of places there, and near there, that have withstood the wear and tear of time, and remind us of Haran. They will be alluded to in another place.

When Heber entered Ireland, he was welcomed by a company of Druids and ladies of the race and name of Lughaid, or Lud, the brother of Arphaxad. The Ludites are described in Nennius as "*a great rolling wave;*" and their descendants are known in the British Islands by the comparatively modern names of Lloyd, Loyd, Luard and Loudon, in Wales and Ireland; McLeod, or sons of Lud, in Scotland. This race of Lud extended over a considerable portion of western Europe :—the old name of Lyons was Lugdunum; Lugdunensis that of Normandy; Mane-Lud, near Loc-Maria-Ker in Armorica, is a place that is remarkable for its megalithic remains, sculptured with the same kind of characters found on stones in several parts of Ireland. Then we have Ludlow, Ludwig, Ludborough, Luddendenfoot, Ludgate, and the old name for the City of London, *Caer-Lud*, which is that of one of the three seats of the Arch-Druids of Britain.*

Perhaps one of the oldest customs on record is the annual tribute to her Majesty the Queen, of "twenty pounds in gold," from Aberfrew (Anglesea), levied by Lud, who is said to have been the Arch-Druid, or king, and founder of London.† Although the account is interesting, we can only give it here in an abbreviated form :—

"The king of London shall be entitled to three tributes :—a tribute of gold from Aberfrew, amounting to twenty pounds ; a tribute in honey from Dinevor, amounting to four tons ; and a tribute of oatmeal from Powis Wynva, of four tons."—*Iolo MSS.*, p. 449.

It is not known to us when the tribute of honey, from Dinevor, was discontinued, nor when the oatmeal, from Powis Wynva, ceased to be carried to London, but this we can say, that even as late as last year the tribute of gold was collected by her Majesty's agent of

* *Cær-Lud* was London ; *Cær-Evroc*, York ; and *Cær-Lleon*, which yet retains its name, is in Monmouthshire.

† About 1008 years B.C., the city of London, it is recorded by Geoffrey of Monmouth and others, was re-built, and re-named Lud, after the destruction of *Cær-Troite*, which is supposed by some to have been built on the site of the present London.

Woods and Forests, now residing at Caernarvon.* The Dinevor above referred to is still in existence, and, no doubt, can be identified as the Dinhabah of Genesis xxxvi. 32, and Chron. i. 43.

If Ireland was Ur, we must show some analogy between its Druidical religion and that of Genesis.

First, then, in order to clear the way for the introduction of more detailed matter illustrative of the people, antiquities, and literature of Ireland, and its primitive faith, we present to our readers' judgment a view of what is written about the principal—at least, the most conspicuous—monuments of Ireland, and their connection with pre-Christian belief there—we mean the Round Towers.

The substance of what is thought about these towers is that they may be African or Phœnician towers, or towers of Persian or Chaldæan Magi. That is to say, they may have been towers for celestial observation, sorcerers' towers, fire towers of

---

* A year or two ago, because the purpose of collecting this tax was not generally understood by the people of Aberfrew, the purpose of collecting it was not generally known—it was forgotten, no doubt—they refused to continue payment until summoned or threatened to be summoned by the Commissioners of Woods and Forests.

a restored Zoroasterian faith ; or they may have been, according to the incredulous Petrie, structures erected by the side of Christian churches. ˋ

We give a passage from the learned Dr. Lanigan, who, although quoted by Petrie with great respect, is left steering a safe middle-course between Mr. Petrie's scepticism and Gen. Vallancey's fanciful learning. Dr. Lanigan says :   ̠

"The great similarity of those towers in the interior of Hindustan to our Irish Round Towers has convinced me that . . . . this mode of architecture was introduced into Ireland in the times of paganism. . . . . The patterns from which the construction of our towers was imitated were most probably the fire-temples of the Persians and others who followed the Magian religion as reformed by Zerdusht, or, as he is usually called, Zoroastres. Those temples were usually round, and some of them were raised to a great height. That fire was in pagan times an object of worship, or, at least, great veneration, in Ireland. and particularly the sun, which was considered the greatest of all fires, is an indubitable fact. Now, the lower part of an Irish Round Tower might have answered very well for a temple—that is, a place in

which was an altar, on which the sacred fire was
preserved, while the middle floors could have served
as habitations for the persons employed in watching
it.   The highest part of the Tower was an observatory,
intended for celestial observations, as I think evidently
appears from the four windows being placed directly
opposite the four cardinal points.

" The veneration in which the pagan Irish held the
heavenly bodies, and especially the sun, must have led
them to apply to astronomical pursuits, which were
necessary also for determining the length of their
years, the solstitial and equinoctial times, and the
precise periods of their annual festivals.   I find it
stated that the doors of most of these towers face the
west.   If this be correct it will add an argument to
show that they contained fire-temples, for the Magians
always advanced. from the west side to worship the
fire.   According to this hypothesis the Round Towers
existed in Ireland before churches were built.   I see
no reason to deny that they did, and the particular
style of their construction shows that they are very
ancient.   But then, it is said, how does it happen
that they are usually found near old churches?   In
the first place, this is not universally true.   Secondly,

it is to be observed that these towers used to be built in towns or villages of some note, such, in fact, as required churches in Christian times. Thus, wherever there was a Round Tower, a church was afterwards erected, but not *vice versâ*; whereas there were thousands of churches in Ireland without any such towers in the vicinity of them. Thirdly, there was a prudential motive for the teachers of Christian faith to build churches near the site of the Round Towers, that they might thereby attract their new converts to worship the true God in the very places where they had been in the practice of worshipping the sun and fire. It may be that some of those towers were built after the establishment of Christianity in Ireland for penitential purposes, as already alluded to, although I have some doubts about it; but I think it can scarcely be doubted that the original models according to which they were constructed belong to the times, of paganism, and that the singular style of architecture which we observe in them was brought from the East, between which and this country it is certain that there was an intercourse at a very ancient period of time."— *Eccl. Hist.*, vol. iv., pp. 406—408.

There can be no doubt that the towers in the interior of Hindostan bear more than a striking likeness to those remaining in Ireland. These resemblances are to be found in such great quantities in the latter place, that it is impossible but to believe Ireland was the centre from which a great deal of the religion of *Budh* developed. This will not appear strange when we consider, in connection with the point, that many of the saints of Ireland bear Aryan and Semetic names. Thus we have :

St. Dagan . Dagon, the God of the Philistines.

St. Molach . The Idol Moloch.

St. Di(*ch*)ul . Devil, in Irish.

St. Satan . Satan, the Destroyer.

St. Cronan . Cronos, the Titan.

St. Bolcain . The Vulcan of Mythology.

St. Ciaran . Chiron, the Centaur.

St. Nessan . Nessus, the Centaur.

St. Declan . Declain, the God of Generation (Irish).

St. Luan . Luan, the Moon.

St. Dererca . Dair-eirce, the Oak of the Ark.

St. Dairmaid Dair-maide, the Branch of the Oak.

Keane says of these names, and referring to many other that could be quoted here, did our space permit : " In my opinion all these names . . can be traced to heathen derivations, and there are many besides which are only Latinized modifications."

Much of the ancient literature of Ireland was destroyed by the early Christians.* They found it *necessary* in many cases to preserve to the Christianized Irish the names of many of the gods and heroes of their forefathers. If not, how are we to account for the inheritance of such names of saints as given above ? But there are hundreds of the kind peculiar to Ireland.

We must agree with Dr. Lanigan that the pagan Irish venerated the sun and heavenly bodies so much that they must have been well practised in astronomical pursuits, and so determined the length of their years, the solstitial and equinoctial times, and the exact periods of their annual festivals. As to there having been intercourses between the East and Ireland at a very ancient period of time there cannot be the slightest doubt, but that the patterns of the towers were brought from the East, westward through Europe, and into Ireland, is more than we are prepared to believe on the authority of those who have preferred

* St. Patrick caused more than 180 volumes of ancient Irish theology to be burned.

E

to find the birth of Archaicism anywhere but in Europe. Why are there not among the hundreds of millions of people of the East, who should be supposed to have preserved some such fire-towers, monuments of their primitive faith, such reminders of it as are to be found in Ireland? The thousands of miles of country and continent they travelled over in Europe and Asia must have to an extent dissipated their original belief, just as the new contacts they experienced must have exercised their intelligence; accelerated by different temperatures, exigencies of living, &c. To the unprejudiced scholar and thinker (not necessarily the man who has studied the languages, antiquities, and comparative mythology of Europe), the Celt has left an eternal register of his occupancy there, corresponding beyond doubt with the Shinar of the Bible, and consequently the Chaldæa and Ur of that Book.

Beside the numerous Round Towers of Ireland there are quantities of stone remains there that must have originated with the people of Genesis. These stone remains have often particular reference to the Assyrian and Egyptian periods, and will be found to have great value in showing how Christianity has retained, often without our knowing, many of the emblems and forms of faith distinctly traceable to a pre-historic, but certain Aryan, and Semitic, and Hamitic source, just as the Irish language has the equivalents of hundreds of its words in Sanskrit, Hebrew, Arabic, and other languages, until lately believed to have had no affinity with one another, and of course no affinity with Irish. In like manner, they would have been thought dreamers who, in a less enlightened age than the present, proposed to show that the origin of many of the Ninevite, Babylonian, and Egyptian monuments is referable to Western Europe.

Bryant, Keane, Hislop, and others call the early stone remains of Europe Cuthite. But they may be proven to have had their origin principally with the posterity of Shem and Japhet, who must have been the first inhabitants of Europe, as not. only their monuments testify, but the names there of places and people to the present day.

Many architectural stone ornaments of Nineveh, India, and Egypt—even in some cases the ancient American architectural stone ornaments*—have (in some cases exact) resemblance to those found in Ireland.

* See Keane's Towers and Temples of Ireland, p. 285.

The symbols of the Archaic kings, prophets, and priests were, as a matter of course, remembered by the people, and reproduced by them wherever they went ; this will account for modification in form, as it does for the relationship of the symbols. . Noah, for instance, was recollected in connection with the Deluge, and consequently, after a time, was venerated as the fish-god Dagon, under the form of a fish, to be found on the cave and other stones of Scotland and Ireland,* resembling the Dagon † of the Philistines and Babylonians. This symbol is also to be found in Egypt and in China.

Perhaps of all the symbols that go to show, an intimate connection between the Celt, the Hebrew, and the Chaldæan, none is more ancient, and at the same time truthful, than the Cross, commonly sup- posed to have taken its significance from Calvary. That this notion is erroneous the next few pages will show.

---

* See The Sculptured Stones of Scotland, by Stuart, and Marcus Keane's Towers and Temples of Ancient Ireland.
† See St. Dagon mentioned, p. 48.

CHAPTER VI.

THE cross as a symbol is traceable to the crossed-rods of the Chaldæan shepherd kings. These symbols are found all over the three kingdoms, especially in Ireland, Scotland, Wales, and Cornwall. The cross is as ancient as the fish and the serpent signs, and as the ring and cup cuttings to be seen on the stones of Scotland and Ireland.

Beside the cross being found upon Egyptian, Babylonian and Assyrian monuments, we find it was worshipped in Mexico ages before the introduction of Christianity. "Large stone crosses," says Prescott, in his "Conquest of Mexico," Vol. i., p. 242, "being erected, probably to the god of rain." Colonel Wilford, in his "Asiatic Researches," Vol. x., p. 124, alluding to the cross, says : "Though it is not an object of worship among the Baud'has, or Buddhists, it is a favourite emblem and device among them ; it is exactly the cross of the Manicheans, with leaves and flowers springing from it." Mr. Morris, in his "Indian

Antiquities,"* notices the Druid and the cross. He
says :—

" It is a fact, not less remarkable than well attested,
that the Druids in their groves were accustomed to
select the most stately and most beautiful tree as an
emblem of the deity they adored, and, having cut the
side branches, they affixed two of the largest of them
to the highest part of the trunk, in such a manner
that those branches extended on each side, like the
arms of a man, and, together with the body, presented the appearance of a *huge cross*; and on the
bark, in several places, was also inscribed the letter
Tau "—the tau-cross.

As we find that the Christian emblem was general
among the Druids, no one need fear assigning to
many of the crosses of Ireland and Scotland a period
far anterior to the introduction of Christianity.

Evidently the inhabitants of Erin, previous to the
arrival of St. Patrick, were well acquainted with the
cross as a symbol of the realization of a hope (we
are not attributing their acquaintance with the cross
to the knowledge they undoubtedly had of Christianity
before St. Patrick's time), impressed upon them, pro-

* Vol. iv., p. 49.

bably for ages, by their Druids and teachers. When the Apostle of Ireland went there, the people believed him, for he taught no new doctrine; he only brought them knowledge that *the* sacrifice was complete in the person of the Son of God: accordingly the fire of their altars was put out, and serpent veneration died away.

The same effect was produced upon the people of Britain, when St. Augustine landed in Thanet; he came bearing a silver crucifix above him, and his companions around singing litanies, upon which the people fell on their knees, and believed the Gospel.

St. Andrew's cross, in a like way, was the sign accepted by the Culdees of Scotland.

The "Men of Israel," Bran, Cfyn, Iltyd, and Fagan, who returned from Rome in the year 57 A.D. to Wales, brought intelligence, by the sign of the cross, of the Redeemer crucified, and the fulfilment of the prophecy of Joel; and they were accordingly acknowledged by the Welsh as veracious teachers.

When the cross *returned* to Chaldæa and Ur, and the adjacent countries, from the East, the people had no difficulty in accepting it. These few remarks, we hope, are sufficient to show that the *cross* is much older than is generally believed.

CHAPTER VII.

THE SONS OF NOAH AND THEIR DESCENDANTS.

THE orthodox teachers tell us that Noah sometime
after his release from the Ark "planted a vine,"
but where he planted the vine is left to conjecture.
There is a great man mentioned in Welsh tradition
called Hu the Mighty, and this Hu, for other reasons
besides having planted a vineyard in Gascony, is by
the Welsh believed to be identical with Noah. It is
true that Hu does not sound very like Noah, but the
same may be said of the Chaldæan Noah, who is
called Xisuthrus. Whether Hu-Gadern, according
to the Triads, the leader of three pacific tribes of
the families of Shem, Ham, and Japhet was the
same person as Noah, Dwy-Van, and Nud, is not to
be perhaps satisfactorily proven; but we will not try
to prove it, for we wish only to show that Celtic
tradition points to the mariners of the Ark as having
been with the first state of things in Western Europe,

and the actual originators of Asiatic kingdoms, subsequent to their sojourn in Europe, particularly in the British Islands. Just because the Irish and Welsh are in the habit of tracing their genealogies up to Noah, so are the Hebrews accustomed. We do not mean to say that these genealogies are entirely to be relied upon; we are only now alluding to one of the Celtic customs being common to the Hebrew. There was no particular and enduring distinction between him and the Celt.

Ancient Britain and Ireland we assume to have been places of sojourn of Noah and his sons, therefore the religion of the Hebrews may reasonably be expected to have been the same as that of the Druids. There are, to the present day, families of the name of Noah to be found in England. Of course some might say— this is no uninterrupted inheritance of the name, only a coincidence to be explained by many causes other than a distinct Noacic source. But it is quite probable, because the Hebrews and the Celts were once the same, that the name has remained here. The name *Hu* (or *Hugh*, as it is now spelled), according to the Welsh, the other name for Noah, is to be counted by thousands in the three kingdoms. No

one is bold enough to affirm that this name is a
foreign importation—Roman, Danish, or Saxon.   The
name is to be found as Hugh, Hughes, Ap-Hugh,
Mac-Hua, and Pugh.

SECTION I.—JAPHET.

The seven sons of Japhet—Gomer, Magog, Madai,
Javan, Elisha, Tarshish, and Dodanam, are traced
by Josephus into Europe.   He shows that their
habitations were situated as follows:—" Beginning
at the mountains Taurus and Amanus, they proceeded
along Asia as far as the river Tanais, and along Europe
to Cadiz, and settling themselves on the lands which
they light upon, which none had inhabited before,
they called the nations by their own names, for
Gomer founded those whom the Greeks now call
Galatians (Galls), but were then called Gomerites.
Magog founded those that from him were named
Magogites, but who are by the Greeks called Scythians.   Now as to Javan and Madai, the Sons of
Japhet, from Madai came the Madeans, who are
called Medes by the Greeks, but from Javan, Ionia,
and all the Grecians are derived.   Thobel founded
the Thobelites, who are now called Iberes, and the

Mosocheni were founded by Mosoch, now they are Cappadocians. . . . . . Of the three sons of Gomer, Aschanax founded the Aschanaxians, who are now called by the Greeks, Rheginians. So did Ripath found the Ripheans, now called Paphlagonians, and Thrugramma, the Thrugrammeans, who, as the Greeks resolved, were named Phrygians. Of the three sons of Javan also, the son of Japhet, Elisa gave name to the Eliseans, who were his subjects, they are now the Æolians. Tharsus, to the Tharsians; for so was Cilicia of old called, the sign of which is that the noblest city they have, and a metropolis also, is Tarsus, the *Tau*, being by change put for Theta."* Because this account seems to us to reconcile with truth a good deal of what we have advanced in support of the names of places and people mentioned in the Old Testament being traceable through Europe, so we would leave it without comment, did it not, in our opinion, require to be viewed with a caution that comes of what we conceive to be more correct—the sons of Shem and Ham were with the sons of Japhet, or before, or

---

* Antiq. of the Jews, Chap. VI., Book I., Sect. I.

shortly after them, in Europe, whence they, in part, entered Asia. More of this after.

If Japhet was, as we cannot doubt, the elder son of Noah, his family may be taken to be the oldest in the world—so the Celtic, or Irish, or Cymric language (which could not then have changed much), and the manners, customs, and the antiquities of Europe, are the oldest in the world.

The most ancient Greek and Roman writers agree to allow the Celts, or Cymry, or Gomeridæ,* to have been *the* primogenital family.

South of the Caucasian range we find that the Cimry were called Gomrai. So it may be that the name Crimea is a corruption of the word Cimry. It is alleged by some that this section of the Cimry allied themselves with the children of Madai, and became the Medes of history; and that another portion of them, separating from the main body, became " Parthwys,"† who in process of time became

---

* These names, along with Irish, Erse, Scotch, &c., mean nearly the same thing. We have before indicated that the Greeks never called the Scythians Celts, Gomerians, or Magogians, hence these names are handed down to us in considerable haze. But they called the sons of Gomer, Gauls.

† *Parthu* in Welsh means to *separate*.

the Parthians, or later Persians. Another division of this people, moving along the chain of the Appenines, became the Cymbri, or Humbri, or Umbri of Italy. These were the main stock from which the Roman confederacy was formed, made up of Latin, Samnite, Sabine, Marsi, and other nations. The Saturnian, or " *Golden Age,*" was during the Umbrian empire of Italy 1200 B.C. The patriarchs of Umbria, both regal and priestly, became the gods of Roman mythology. The termination of words in Celtic and Latin differ, but it is curious how the root forms of the Latin are discoverable to be Celtic. The proper names of the oldest Latin families are formed on a Celtic basis, thus:—Claudius, Catullus, Cato, Pompeius, Lucullus, Camillus, Marcus, &c. The sewers of Umbrian Rome, and the cyclopian fortresses and temples were erected by Umbrian kings. The religion of the Umbrians was the druidical or patriarchal. The Tuscan or Etrurian empire followed, and was composed of the same Celtic element. The Etrurian may be said to have given way to the Gallic irruptions of Brennus and Belinus.

From the very earliest times the country of the descendants of Gomer was known as Gallacia.

" For Gomer founded those whom the Greeks now (Josephus' time) call Galatians (Galls)."

The most remarkable portions of the Gallacia, alluded to by Josephus, were Caledonia, or Galedonia, and Gaul, and the province of Gallacia in Spain. The Welsh of the present day pride themselves upon being sons of Gomer. There are many families of the name in England, but they are chiefly to be found in Wales.

MAGOG.—It is not only General Vallancey that makes allusion to the Irish being descendants of Magog; there is frequent mention made of this fact in the history and tradition of Ireland. Magog, or *Son of the North*, as his name signifies, is in many Scripture references associated with the Isles of the Sea.

JAVAN.—Another son of Japhet is Javan. The *Ja* modified into E in Welsh, the name becomes Evan or Evans, one of the most numerous family names in Wales.

ASHKENEZ.—This Galatian (son of Gomer) has been traced to Germany. Ascanians the ancient Germans were called, and known as such by the Saxons. Askenes is yet a proper name in Germany.

RIPPATH.—This other son of Gomer, like Javan or

Evan, seems to have bequeathed his name nearly in an unaltered form to the present Griffiths of Wales.

TOGAMAH.—The people of "Togamah and his bands," invariably associated with Gog and Magog, are the people of the northern quarters—Scandinavia, and particularly Russia.*

ELISAH.—Elisah was the son of Javan. Josephus says he gave name to the Eliseans, who were his subjects. They became the Æolians. The Eleusinian Mysteries originated with the sons of Elisah. To turn to the name as it is found in the British Islands, there are people called Elisah, or as the Welsh give it, Elias; hence the names Ellis, Ellison, &c. Elisah and Elias were favourite names with the Hebrews, as may be seen in 1 Kings xvii. 6, and xix. 16. In Ezek. xxii. 7, there is mention made of the "Isles of Elisah."

TARSHISH.—Another son of Javan was Tarshish. That that portion of Iberia (Spain) called Tarshish was named from this son of Javan, Josephus, as we have shown, believes. When Josephus wrote, Tarshish

---

* "The orientals hold," says D'Herbelot, *Bibl. Orient.*, p. 722, "that Japhet had a son called *Rous*, not mentioned by Moses, who peopled Russia."

must have been, from his remarks, a place of some note. But the Bible references to it prove this :— "Silver, spread into plates, is brought into Tarshish" (Jer. x. 9) ; "Tarshish was thy merchant with iron" (Ezek. xxvii. 12) ; " The ships of Tarshish shall sing of thee (Tyre), in thy market" (Ezek. xxvii. 25) ; "And Jonah rose up to flee unto Tarshish" (Jonah i. 3) ; "All King Solomon's drinking vessels were of gold, and all the vessels of the house of the forest of Lebanon were of pure gold; none were of silver : it was nothing accounted of in the days of Solomon. For the king had at sea a navy of Tarshish . . . . . . once in three years came the navy of Tarshish, bringing gold, and silver, ivory, and apes, and peacocks." (1 Kings, x., 21, 22.)

DODANAM.—This, the last son of Javan, and a Galatian, seems not to have left his name so as to be clearly discerned in these times. Nevertheless it is capable of fair interpretation. Isaiah says :—"O ye travelling companies of Dedanim," (xxi. 13,) with evident reference to a nomad, but yet semi-civilized, people, who, several centuries before this, settled in Ireland, called Tuath-de-Danaan.

The sons of Japhet, as we have shown, are

constantly referred to in the Prophets as the "in-habitants of the isles," and in Gen. v. 10 we find :—
"By these were the isles of the Gentiles divided in their lands, every one after his tongue, after their families in their nations."

CHAPTER VIII.

THE SONS OF HAM, AND HIS DESCENDANTS IN
WESTERN EUROPE — PROPHESY AGAINST THE
"ISLES," AND RETROSPECT OF HABAKKUK.

THE evidence that the children of Noah dwelt
together before the division in the time of Peleg,
is sufficient to warrant our looking for traces of this
son of Noah in the country of Gomer's posterity.
Ham is described as the father of Canaan. The
word Ham, which abounds in the British Islands
in the names of localities and families, almost identifies the "isles of the sea" as a portion of the
Hamath of Isaiah (x. 9).

The city of Hammonah, and the valley of Hammon Gog, with which it is mentioned in Ezek. xxxix.,
was situated in these islands. The word Gog is
associated with places in Britain. Hammon Gog,
interpreted through the Welsh, means literally
Northampton; Gog means *north*, and Ham bears
its own signification. According to some of the

old maps, an example of which is appended to Dr. Skene's edition of the " Four Ancient Books of Wales," *Prydian-y-Gogledd* means the northern division of Britain. The north of England, including the lowlands of Scotland, was at one time in possession of the Welsh, which may account for this distinction being preserved. North-men are called *Gwr-y-Gogledd*, or the men of the north—so the Norwegian, Norse-man, and Norman—the latter name being given to the men of the north of France who went there under Rollo the Dane.

In some parts of England the word Ham is yet preserved by itself—Ham, in Glamorganshire, and East and West Ham, near London. Again, we have North and South *Ham*pton, *Ham*stead, in Staffordshire, *Ham*pton, near London ; and names of people, *Ham*, *Ham*pson, *Ham*mon, *Ham*mond, *Ham*mich, and perhaps *Ham*ilton.*

Ham was the father of Canaan. A place derived of this name is Canna, one of the islands of the Hebrides—perhaps the Canneh of Ezek. xxviii. 23,

* The Hamiltons quarter a ship on their shields, the ship of Nevidd or Hu. In the Iolo MSS. it is stated that Japhet was the first to bear a *targe* with a boat on it, in memory of the Deluge, and the saving of his family from the flood.

mentioned in connection with Eden and Haram ? *Cain*-Mawr, a mountain in North Wales, seems also to have retained the name. As to the names of people there are many : Cain, Kean, Keane, Kane, Kaine, Kain, Du Cane, Cann, &c.

The son of Canaan was Cush. There are some who believe that there are traces of Cush in Ireland. The supposed Cuthite remains there are considered by antiquaries to be of great importance towards the elucidation of a great prehistoric people. Cushandal and Cushenden, both in Ireland, are with Midian, or Madian, spoken of in Habk. iii. 7, and they are to be identified as the Cushan and Midian of Habakkuk. Cushandal is in the neighbourhood of the Accads. The old name for Meath, according to Irish authorities, was Midhe or Midian.* Cushandal†

---

* The name in Irish is Midhe, pronounced *Me*, and Latinised Midii and Midensis, and Anglicised Midians, and sometimes Mithians. The kingdom of Meath comprised the present counties of Meath, Westmeath, with parts of Longford, King's County, Dublin, and Kildare. The kingdom was in after times added to the province of Leinster.

† Cushandal and Cushenden are, according to Lewis's Topography of Ireland, within three miles of each other, on the Antrim coast. Cushingtown is also mentioned, as a district or union comprising Carnagh, Ballyane, Tallyrath, and old Ross.

is situated near Meath, but may not have been a part of the old Meath province of Ireland. Teman (Temora) may also have been situated there.

In connection with Cush we now refer more generally to Ireland :

Inspirational utterances in the forms of visions of the past, as well as prophesies, distinguish Ezekiel, Isaiah, and Habakkuk.

Their prophesies were not more remarkable than their retrospections. The words of Habk. iii. 2—7, are an example of retrospect. The prophesies against the Isles had been fulfilled, and he sublimely says :—

" God came from Teman, and the Holy One from Mount Paran. Selah. His glory covered the heavens, and the earth was full of his praise.

" And his brightness was as the light ; he had horns coming out of his hand : and there was the hiding of his power.

" Before him went the pestilence, and burning coals went forth at his feet.

" He stood and measured the earth : he beheld and drove asunder the nations, and the everlasting mountains were scattered, the perpetual hills did bow : his ways are everlasting. I saw the tents of *Cushan* in affliction ; and the curtains of the land of *Midian* did tremble.

" Was the Lord displeased against the rivers ? Was thine anger against the rivers ? Was thy wrath against the sea that thou didst ride upon thine horses and thy chariots of salvation ?

" Thy bow was made quite naked, according to the oaths of the tribes, even thy word. Selah. Thou didst cleave the earth with rivers.

" The mountains saw thee, and they trembled : the overflowing of the water passed by : the deep uttered his voice and lifted up his hands on high.

" The sun and moon stood still in their habitation : at the light of thine arrows they went, and at the shining of thy glittering spear.

" Thou didst march through the land in indignation : thou didst thresh the heathen in anger."

We have quoted Habakkuk to this length, because there is much more in his words than the sublime.

Geologists speak of disturbed formations, for they find the primitive rocks uppermost, and the great mystery of the formation of the Irish bog has never yet been solved. Vast deposits, miles in extent, of dark vegetable and animal matter, containing forests

of oak, and other trees with burnt charred roots, many
in a horizontal position, would seem to tell of the fire
of the Lord, and remind us of the burning coals that
went forth at his feet. Strange bones of men and
animals, oak canoes, jewels bearing strange characters,
gold and silver ornaments in great quantity are found
in these deposits, and assure us of a great earthquake
having occurred there. The loughs, the mountains,
the great caves, of which Fingal's is but one, tell
us of a convulsion which the Scripture records treat
of over and over again. The Bible reminds us of
several earthquakes, one of the most remarkable is
that which was in the twenty-seventh year of Isaiah,
king of Judah, B.C. 787. Zechariah and Amos speak
of it. It is recorded in the annals of Ulster that an
earthquake at one time overthrew over fifty-six of the
Round Towers.

"Drove asunder the nations," says Habakkuk;
may it not be that the allusion here is to the British
Islands, cut from the Continent of Europe? Look
at the map of Europe, and while remembering the
kindred races of the French, Spanish, *Old British*,
Welsh, Irish, and the Erse, and the antiquities of each,
it is impossible but to be struck with the words of

the prophet, "Was thine anger against the rivers?
Was thy wrath against the sea?" These are words
that follow the description of Cushan in affliction,
and the trembling of the land of Midian. Who
can say they were not intended to describe the
separation of Great Britain and Ireland from the
mainland of the Continent by the interposition of
river and sea?*

* The following note is appended to the part translation, by
Owen Connellan, of the Annals of The Four Masters. It
illustrates the Welsh variation given in the Iolo MSS. :—

"*Eruption of Lakes.*—Accounts are given by our ancient
annalists of great lakes in various parts of Ireland having suddenly burst forth in very remote times; and in Ulster the
following are the chief instances recorded :—More than a thousand years before the Christian era, Lough Foyle, in Derry, is
said to have burst forth, overflowed the adjoining plain, and
drowned in its waves Feabhal, or Feval, the son of Lodan, one
of the Tuath-De-Danan chiefs, from whom it was called Lough
Feval, now Lough Foyle. About eight centuries before the
Christian era, in the reign of Fiacha Labhruine, one of the
Milesian monarchs, it is stated by all our annalists, that the
great lake, called Loch Saimer, afterwards Lough Erne, suddenly
burst forth, and overwhelmed an immense tract of land, called
Magh Geannain, or the plain of Geannan, which was so named
from the plain of Geannan, one of the Firbolg kings."

————

A description of "*Bogs and Ancient Forests*" is here given,
to shew that the trees, of old, indigenous to the Irish soil,
have been discovered in these places, with burnt trunks and

"Alafon, the son of Brywlais, was a very kind king in word and action, and also a bard of transcendant compositions. A tremendous earthquake occurred in

roots; but we differ from the author in the cause he assigns for their appearance.

"*Bogs and Ancient Forests.*—In various parts of Ulster are extensive moors and wild heaths, famous for hares, grouse, and other game. The bogs in the different counties are numerous and extensive, and in the whole of the province estimated to contain about two or three hundred thousand acres. These bogs are chiefly composed of the remains of ancient forests of oak, pine or fir, yew, ash, alder, birch, hazel, thorn, willow, &c., which covered the entire of the country in remote times. Oak forests particularly abounded in Ireland in ancient times, and the Irish oak was so very durable, that it was found superior to that of any other country for ship-building, timber for houses, furniture, and various other purposes.

"In our old historians are accounts of the clearing of many great plains, and the cutting down of forests in various parts of Ireland in the earliest ages, some of them more than a thousand years before the Christian era. In the clearing out of these great plains the forests were destroyed, and great quantities of trees are found deeply buried in the bogs; and in the formation of the grand canal, when cutting through the bog of Allen, in Kildare, oak, fir, yew, and other trees, were found buried twenty or thirty feet below the surface, and these trees generally lie prostrated in a horizontal position, *and have the appearance of being burned at the bottom of their trunks and roots*, fire having been found far more powerful in prostrating those forests than cutting them down with the axe; and the great depth at which these trees are found in bogs, shews that they must have lain there for many ages."—*Connellan, A. F. M.*, 337.

his time, until the mountains and rocks were rent, and the rivers, being diverted from their beds, ran through the chasms of the ground." This is a paragraph from the Iolo MSS.; and the note upon the earthquake mentioned in it, is subjoined :—

"Cambro-British traditionary records commemorate many violent convulsions of the earth, that seem to have occurred too far back in antiquity to admit of any chronological computation of their real periods : still, other testimonies, aided by natural appearances and geological comparisons, frequently tend to verify those immemorial events. Druidical mythology (Welsh Prize Essay on the Cœlbren, p. 7), says, that the ALMIGHTY, when neither life nor being existed save Himself, vocalised his NAME, and consequently, that all animated nature sprang simultaneously to light and life, at the ineffably melodious sound, thus transmitting to futurity a magnificent reference to the creation. The awful bursting of the *lake of Floods* that deluged the world, and drowned all living things except Dwyfan and Dwyfach (the man and woman of God), who escaped in 'the Bald Ship,' and by their offspring re-peopled the world, is another recorded tradition of the deluge (13 Hist. Tri.), which is sustained by an additional Celtic version of that event, that probably appertained to the aborigines of the island; for among ' *The Three Arduous Works of the Island of Britain,*' is named :—' The ship of Nefydd, Lord of Lords, that carried in it a male and female of every living creature, when the lake of Floods burst.' (97th Triad.) The mighty occurrences thus recorded, would, probably, have only been retained as the imaginings of erratic genius, were they not elucidated by the Mosaic accounts, independently of the mythologies, in varied forms, of perhaps all other nations, kindreds, and tongues of the earth.

" In nearer association with the effects of the *earth-quake*, attributed in the text to this reign, may be quoted the 67th Triad : ' The three subordinate islands of the island of Britain—the isle of Orkney (*Orc*), the isle of Man, and the isle of Wight. Afterwards the land was so rent by the sea that Môn (Anglesey) became an island ; and in the same manner Orkney was rent into a multitude of islands ; and other parts of Alban (Scotland) and Cambria became islands.' (E. W.'s trans.) The testimony of this Triad is supported by Mark, the Hermit's copy of Nennius, where the follow-ing passage occurs :—' Tres magnas insulas habet ;

quarum una australis vergit contra armoricas, et vocatur insula guerth. Secunda sita est in umbilico maris inter hiberniam et bryttaniam; et nominatur eubonia vel manau. Tertia est in extremo boreali limite orbis bryttaniæ ultra Pictos et vocatur orch.' (It [Britain] has three great islands, one towards the south, opposite the Armorican shore, called Wight; the second situated mid-sea between Ireland and Britain, called Eubonia or Man; and the third, to the extreme north of the British boundary, beyond the Picts, named Orkney.) An *ancient proverb*, quoted by the same venerable author, as applicable to the rule of the paramount monarchs of the island, affords further corroboration :—'Judicavit Bryttaniam cum tribus insulis.' (He ruled over Britain and its three islands.) From the construction of the foregoing Triad, it is pretty clear that its latter clause is merely a commentary, appended by some remote transcriber, to account for the altered appearance of the Orkneys after the rupture; and we may fairly conclude also, that the Triads were among the *ancient traditions* and *ancient books* from which Nennius professes to have drawn his information—'Ex traditione veterum, ex antiquis libris nostrorum.' The third Triad of the

Hengwrt Series (Myv. Arch. II., p. 2) gives, like the
fac-simile prefixed to Gunn's translation of the His-
toria, twenty-eight as the number of ancient British
cities, although some of the names vary in these
records. Different copies, however, have extended
the number to thirty-three and thirty-five. . . . .

"The extraordinary bed of the Avon, from Bristol to
the Severn, is evidently an immense cleft, formed by
some tremendous convulsion; and Caer-odornant
(the city of the rift river), the Welsh name of that
ancient city seems to support the hypothesis. Whether this rupture was produced by an earthquake,
similar to that recorded in the text, or by volcanic
eruption, cannot now be determined, further than that
the agency of the latter may be rationally inferred
from the proximity of *Brandon*-hill to it. I am
informed by persons who have examined the district, that the *original* course of the Avon, through
Somersetshire, from Nailsey, near Bristol, to its con-
fluence with the Severn at Clevedon, may still be
traced."

The above is appended to the "Genealogy of
Iestyn, the son of Gwrgan, prince of Glamorgan;
together with a short account of the accomplishments

and achievements of the several princes it includes,"
in the Iolo Manuscripts,* pp. 340, 341.

¡ The Psalms, as well as the books of the Prophets,
are full of allusions to this great convulsion, accom-
panied by fire. "A great shaking in the land of
Israel," and "the fire of the Lord," may be understood
as the "disturbed formations," "volcanic actions,"
&c., of the modern geologist.

The Koran refers to the inhabitants of the wood
near Median as having been destroyed ; and of lofty
towers that were thrown down.

The Median referred to is to be distinguished
from the Midian by the Red Sea (which we first hear
of as in existence in the time of Abraham), most likely
named after Midian, the son of Keturah ; Midian, as
we understand it, was the land of the Midianite
merchantmen, who carried tin from Cornwall to
Phœnicia and to other parts of the East.

* "A Selection of Ancient Welsh Manuscripts, in prose and
verse, from the collection made by the late Edward Williams
(IOLO MORGANWG), for the purpose of forming a continuation
of the Myfyrian archæology ; and subsequently proposed as
materials for a new history of Wales : with English translation
and notes, by his son, the late Taliesin Williams (AB IOLO), of
Merthyr Tydfil.   Published for the Welsh MSS. Society."
MDCCCXLVIII.

These Midianites, in company with Ishmaelites, are described in Gen. xxxvii. 25—28 as coming from Gilead with their camels, and bearing spicery, and balm, and myrrh, to Egypt—probably influenced to do so from the family relationship that existed between them; for the brothers of Cush were Mizraim, Phut, and Canaan: Egypt was the land of Mizraim, and Phut and Canaan are considered to have been nearly intermediate places.

The supposed Cuthite remains at Cashel bear striking resemblance to some of the Ninevite sculptures: Nergal, or Nimrod, the winged lion, as exhibited in the British Museum, is a remarkable imitation of the winged lion of Cashel.*

The purpose of our remarks upon the sons of Ham and their descendants in Western Europe, is not to prove that the *genesis* of things was with them there more than with the sons of Japhet, and to an extent the sons of Shem; in fact, all that we have advanced about them goes only so far as to shew that they were in Europe, and left their marks there before going to the East, taking with them the ideas that developed monuments akin to those of the land of the cradle of

* See Kane's "Temples and Towers of Ireland."

their race. The Egyptian, Indian, and Arab monuments have their Celtic art affinities, just as the people of Egypt, India, and Arabia, have Celtic relationship of speech. The principal characteristic of the ancient Irish style of architecture is observable in the architecture of these countries, *viz.*, massive stones laid in irregular courses, and doorways having sloping or inclining jambs.

CHAPTER IX.

CUSH AND NIMROD.

THE most influential and celebrated of the sons of Cush was Nimrod—"the mighty hunter before the Lord," the beginning of whose kingdom was Babel, Erech, Accad, and Calneh. We have reserved from the order of our remarks upon the three latter places, reference to Babel, until we treated of it in connection with Cush and Nimrod.

There can be no doubt that to Semiramis was attributed a good deal of what was actually accomplished by Ninus. The testimony of Megasthenes, as preserved by Abydenus of Tyre, goes to show us that it was by "Belus" Babylon was surrounded with a wall;* although some have represented that it was by Semiramis alone. This Belus may be distinguished from "Bel," who began the City and Tower of Babel—for the reason that we are told Bel had to leave both *unfinished;* if so he

* See Corry's Fragments, pp. 45-6.

G

could not have surrounded the city with a wall.
We may suppose, though, that Ninus, as the
son of Cush, inherited his father's title of "Bel,"
or "the Confounder"—the explanation then is, that
Ninus or Nimrod—for he is called both names in-
differently—was the first to consolidate the Babylonian empire, and that he, like his father Cush, who
must have left among the first Babylonians the im-
pression of his greatness, was deified "Bel," which
word afterwards, in most languages of Europe, took
the form of "Bel*us*."

According to Layard, Rhea or Cybele, the "Tower-
crowned Goddess," and "Goddess of Fortification,"
was a Babylonian Goddess, and the counterpart of the
"Deity presiding over bulwarks and fortresses;"* consequently she originated with the mystical Semiramis,
supposed queen of Nimrod or Ninus.

To us, it is almost unnecessary, in the present
confused st ite of the question as to Semiramis being
the wife of Ninus or Nimrod (and especially as we
have only proposed to treat of certain parts of the
subject in this work), to offer any contribution
towards the solution of the difficulty. However, as

---

* Nineveh and its Remains, Vol. ii. pp. 456, 457.

far as we can judge, it is quite possible that Semiramis was the mother, not wife, of Nimrod or Ninus, and, therefore, the wife of Bel or Cush. The first remains of this Bel are to be found in the tradition, Druidic religion, mythology, stone monuments, &c., of Europe.

Kronos or Saturn was Rhea's husband. Traced back to the original, we find that Kronos was no other than the first king of Babylon, worshipped under the names of Bel and Bal.*

In the genuine copies of Eusebius, there is no mention made of any Belus, actual *king* of Assyria, before Ninus, so, according to that authority, Kronos or Saturn was not only Cush, Bel or Bal, but Ninus or Nimrod. Under the name Kronos, Nimrod is known as king of the Cyclops, who were his brethren,† and "the inventors of tower-building."

What may be in a general way deduced from the foregoing is that, notwithstanding the different names

---

* See upon this point Clericus' *De Philosophia Orientali*, lib. i. sect. ii. cap. 37.

† "The Cyclops . . . were the brethren of Kronos, the father of Jupiter."—The Scholiast on the *Prometheus* of Æschylus, p. 56. And refer to " *Turres, ut Aristotdes, Cyclopes* (invenerunt)." Pliny lib. vii., cap. 56, p. 171.

under which Nimrod is represented, he inherited some of the nature and attributes of Bel or Cush, *the Con-founder*, which entitled him to be deified as his father was ; and that he completed the tower and city of Babel, commenced by his father, who, if he conceived the building of this city and tower, may be fairly accredited with originating "tower-building," the invention of which is sometimes attributed to Nimrod.

This may throw some light upon what are called the Cuthite remains in Ireland, the Round Towers, &c., of that country.

CHAPTER X.

COLONIES of Hyperboreans erroneously called
Cuthites, reached as far as the Mæotis, at the
north of the Euxine Sea, and to the coast of the
Adriatic. They extended their settlements to Asia, and
laid the foundation of the Ninevite and Babylonian
Monarchies. In prehistoric times we have glimpses
of them, as having from the west of Europe gone
northward over Scandinavia, and Scythia in Europe,
(Russia). Many remaining in Umbria, left their
names, afterwards remembered in association with the
Mons Palatinus of Rome. They also went southward from the British Islands (or country of Britain
as an integral portion at one time, perhaps, of the
Continent) to Iberia, (Spain) and Mauritania. Hence
it is easy to conceive how they may have progressed
along the north coast of Africa, making settlements
in conjunction with the sons of Mizraim, and extending their influence into Asia-Minor, Southern Asia, and
Hindostan, the while, of course, mixing and drawing

closer the ties of consanguinity with the people of Phut and Canaan, and Seba and Havilah, Sabta, Raamah, and the other sons of Cush, of whom we know so little, but who must have in Egypt and in Hindostan, with a certain Semitic admixture of race, created civilizations and empires, it may be, as great as the Babylonian and Ninevite, and co-existant with them.

Bryant says of the Hyperboreans :—" They were of the Titanic race, and called Sindi, a name, as I have shown, common among the Cuthites.* The Scindi are one family of those who live upon the Mæotis. Strabo speaks of them as called among other names Sauromatæ. Those who live above the Euxine, Ister, and Adriatic, were formerly called Hyperboreans and Sauromatæ, and Arimaspians. This people were esteemed very sacred,† and it is said that Apollo,

---

* The name might be common among them, but this does not prove the Cuthites Hyperboreans.

† Keane has a note upon this passage :— " With regard to the term sacred, applied to the Hyperboreans, I would remark, that Faber informs us that the original Scythic or Cuthite empire, founded by Nimrod (which composed the Babylonian, Assyrian, and Medo-Persic empire within its limits) was denominated Iran, and that the region is still known by that name among the inhabitants.—(Faber, Vol. iii., p. 377.)

Ireland had the name of *Irin* and *Sacred Island* long before our Lord's advent. Erin, or *Irin*, as Diodorus Siculus calls it :

when he was exiled from Heaven, and had his offspring slain, retired to their country. It seems he

and Iran, Sir John Malcolm informs us, is the term by which
the Persians from the most ancient times call their country.
Avienus, copying from Hamilco and the remote annals of the
Phœnicians, calls it ' *Sacra Insula* ' *as so denominated by the
men of old.*—(O'B., pp. 117 and 120.)"

From these notices Keane concludes that "the original
Cuthite, or Scythic region, was so called (Iran, the sacred
country) from the ark having rested upon its mountain, as well
as from its reputation as the site of Paradise ; and that when
some of the Cuthite Scythians emigrated to Ireland, they
brought with them the name of *Iran*, only changing it to *Irin*,
to express the insular character of their new settlement." The
passage ought to read, "When some of the Hyperboreans
emigrated to the Nimrodian empire—Babylonia, Assyria, Medo-
Persia, they called it Iram, Iran, or Irin, from the country they
left, Iran or Irin, or Erin, the ' *Sacra Insula*,' ' *as denominated
by the men of old*,' according to Avienus, who copied from
Hamilco and the remote annals of the Phœnicians."

It is a pity Keane has found it necessary, with Bryant, in all
cases to make the Hyperboreans Cuthites.

As to *Iran* being changed to *Irin* for the purpose of expressing
the insular character of Ireland, it is less likely than that there
was no island of *Iran* at the time, no Ireland surrounded by
ocean, but simply a district of Iran, or *sacred country*, situated
in western Europe as an integral part of the continent. How is
it that it was necessary to change *Iran* into *Irin*, when we find
the *an* of *Aran* (the name of an island on the west of Scotland,
and of others on the western Irish coast) means *island*, from
innis, an island ? *An* is changed from *in*, and contracted of *innis* ;
so *ar* is contracted of *ard*, high, the high island, or island of
rock.

wept, and there was a tradition that every tear was·
amber."

> ' The *Celtic sages a tradition hold*
> That every drop of amber was a tear
> Shed by Apollo *when he fled* from Heaven,
> For sorely did he weep, and sorrowing, passed
> Through many a doleful region *till he reached*
> *The sacred Hyperboreans.'*
>   Quoted by Bryant from *Apollon Argonaut,* L. 4, v. 611.·

" They are sometimes represented as Arimaspians,.
and their chief Priestesses were named Oupis, Loxo,
and Hecüerge, by whom the *Hyperborean rites are*
said to have been brought to Delos. They never returned,.
but took up their residence and officiated in the island"
(Delos). " *People from the same quarter are said to*
have come to Delphi in Phocis, and to have found
out the oracular seat of Apollo. Pausanias produces
from this the evidence of the ancient Priestess Bæo.·
She makes mention of *Olen, the Hyperborean, as the*
first prophet of Delphi, and further says, that the first
temple of the Deity was founded by him in conjunction with Pagasus and Agyieus. . . . . The Mons·
Palatinus at Rome was supposed to have been
occupied by Hyperboreans. . . . . There was also an
Hyperborean of great fame, called *Abaris, who is*

mentioned by Herodotus. He was the son of Zeuth, styled Seuthes, and is represented as *very knowing in the art of divination,* and gifted with supernatural powers."

Keane also gives what Bryant quotes from Pherenicus (Scholia in Pind. Olymp. Od. 3, v. 28) : "' He sang also of the Hyperboreans, who live in the extremities of the world, under the temple of Apollo, far removed from the din of war. They are celebrated as being of the ancient blood of the Titans, and were a colony placed in this wintry climate by the Arimaspian monarch, the son of Boreas.

" The two most distant colonies of this family westward were upon the Atlantic ocean : *the one in Europe to the north ; the other opposite at the extreme part of Africa.* The country of the latter was Mauratania ; whose inhabitants were the Atlantic Ethiopians. They looked upon themselves as of the same family as the Gods ; and *they were certainly descended from some of the first deified mortals. Those who occupied the Provinces of Iberia* [Spain] *and Baetica, on the other side, went under the same titles, and preserved the same histories as those who have been mentioned before.'* "

And he further remarks :—" Although Ireland seems

never to have entered Bryant's mind as connected with
Cuthite history, every sentence in these quotations
respecting the Hyperboreans—when taken in connection with Irish records—seems to point to Ireland as
the home of that people to whom ancient Greek
authors refer as the Hyperboreans"—p. 235. For
additional information on same subject, he refers
to O'Brien's *Round Towers,* who quotes through
Bryant from Mr. Booth's translation of the notice respecting the *Insula Hyperborea,* by Diodorus Siculus
—pp. 396, 397, O'Brien. And while we agree with
Mr. Keane that "Ireland never entered Mr. Bryant's
mind in connection with Cuthite history," still we
cannot but find fault with the former attributing
everything archaic, everything with Ninevite, Babylonian, and Egyptian resemblances in Ireland to the
descendants of Cush. If we take the word Hyperborean as generally understood, it offers contradiction
to this — *Hyper,* beyond, *Boreas,* north — beyond
Boreas, or the north, *e. g.* an inhabitant of the
north, or the district over which *the descendants of
Japhet* are supposed to have gone — therefore a
people *not Hamitic,* as those of Cush undoubtedly
were. But if, instead of Hyperborean, we read *Heber-*

borean, we are then led to the consideration that of all names of countries not one reminds us so much of Heber and the Hebrew, as *Iberia,* or as it was sometimes spelt *Heberia.* The name of Heber must have been familiar to the Phœnicians, who traded with Tarshish, the country of Heber, who gave his name to Hibernia.

The Greeks must have adopted the word from the Phœnicians, and as the country (or countries) of Heber was to the earlier, indeed to the later Greeks, quite undefined, *beyond* their knowledge, so it is possible, indeed likely, that the word *hyper* (beyond) had undergone a change with the Greeks even before the advent of Cecrops or Cadmus. The latter did not bring the language of the people of the first states of Greece out of Phœnicia, it was to a great extent already being spoken there—he only brought them their alphabet. It may be necessary to offer a conjecture as to how *Boreas* became affixed to the word in question—the *north* of Europe, to the Greeks and Romans, as we hinted before, was as mysterious as the people who wandered there, so mysterious indeed, that a race of and residing in *Western* Europe were called *the Hyperborei* by them.

Boreas is generally explained "The northern wind,"
or "Bellowing wind." Hyperborea was unquestionably the land of the Druid and Bard, whose religion
was identical with that of the later Hebrew. Now, if
we understand that in the Welsh language *p*, *b*, and *t*
are commutable letters,* and in Irish, beside others,
b and *d* (both tongues in this respect simply exemplify-
ing the universal affection of sounds), we have some
light thrown upon *bard*, *druid*, and *bruide* (Irish), as
having been the same in meaning. There is very
little, if any, distinction between the original Bard or
Druid :—

"*Derwydd yw bardd wrth bwyll ansawdd, a gorford,
ac ei swydd yw athrawiaethu.* The *druid is a bard*,
according to the reason, nature, and necessity of things,
and his office is to instruct."—*Barddas*, in Pugh.

If in the Irish and Welsh the term *bard* was
equivalent to *druid*, the Greeks were not astray
in rendering *druid bard*, and if they interpreted
bruide by *boreas*, from that word to their minds signifying as well as "northern" or "bellowing" wind,
the particular locality whence it came to them, they
only used a very natural idiom, one that originated

* Britain, is *Prydian* in Welsh.

perhaps from *bar*, in Celtic (which supplied the first idiom of the Greek), the *top* ; because the *north*, or the region of *Boreas*, to them would appear *away from*, *above*, the *top* ás it were, or north of their country. This view is strengthened by the fact that the Hyperboreans always sent their offerings southward; :so, as we have before noticed, their priestesses .are said to have brought the Hyperborean rites to Delos, and people from their country to have gone to Delphi in Phocis, and discovered the oracular seat of Apollo. If this be admitted, the country of the Hyperborean might with equal reason have been called the country of the *Heber-druids*, or *Heberbards*, the priest-poets, who, according to Pausanias and others, came into Greece, and originated sacrifice and the mysteries of their faith there.

The more the question of the distribution of the first races of mankind is studied, the more we are brought to the belief of the impossibility of arriving at anything certain as to where the sons of Noah remained longest in Europe. Yet no one who has looked for particulars, and thought about the dispersion of Noah's family, but must be struck with evidences of their having been in Europe together.

But judge by language and mythology, physical and psychological characteristics, by monumental stones, or fossil remains; and, separated from the *necessity* of pre-judgment, we must be convinced by the over-whelming testimony in favour of the SONS of Noah and their families having both settled and sojourned in Europe. Look north, south, east and west, from Pole to Pole, over Europe, Asia, America, and again Europe, speech, faith, hope, superstition, joy, and fear, inscribed stone and laboured ornament, city, empire, prosperity, decline, and each emphatically proves the universal affinity of nations, and of people and their handiworks.

Shem was the father of all the sons of Heber, and we cannot possibly perceive how Iberia could have taken its name, unless it was from Heber, or some one of his sons of the same name. The old Iberians were undoubtedly of the same race as the Hebrew, and whether they be called *Celtic*, in common with those of the British Islands and Gaul, or not, it makes little matter, for the old Chaldæan institutions, ceremonies, &c., were Druidical; or conversely, if it be preferred, the old *Druidical* institutions, ceremonies, &c., were Chaldæan.

CHAPTER XI.

THE sons of Shem were Elam, Asshur, Arphaxad, Lud, and Aram. The traces of them are numerous in Western Europe. Like the Cuthite and Japhetian, these are to be found in the comparison of their language, names of people and places, monumental art remains, &c. The names of people are perhaps as good evidence, if we except the names of places which endure longest uncorrupted, as can be produced in proof of a Semetic occupancy of Europe. The chief consideration then, is to show how these remains are discoverable in the quarter indicated, in a proportion that sets down as trifling what has been referred to in favour of Shem and his children distributing themselves over southern Asia prior to the settlement of Europe.

There are fewer traces of the Elamites and the people of Asshur to be found in Europe, although they must have proceeded in their easterly course through it. It is not a little interesting to contemplate the pastoral staff or crook which is yet to be seen on their monuments; and the winged bull, or Asshur the traveller—suggested, as some believe, by the wings of the bull, just as the winged lion already referred to symbolized the "mighty hunter,"—and think of thousands of years that have gone over the efforts of man, leaving almost untoothed links that prove the present but the sequence of his most remote existence.* The people of Elam and Asshur took with them the remembrance of the Deluge, which they have so well assisted in sending down to posterity in writing. The *Asshurbani-pal,* so frequently represented in the stone remains of Asia, means literally in Irish—*Asshur of the white pall, or mantle,* identifying him with the white-robed priests, or Druids.

ARPHAXAD.—If Noah was represented under the form of a fish, Arphaxad was in Chaldæa under that

---

* The cow, or bull, symbolizes the Semetic people of whom was Abraham, referred to in the book of Enoch as a "white cow." The "sacred cow" of India, as well as their "tree and serpent" suggests relationship to the Assyrians and Europeans. Europa and the Bull almost mean—mythic accounts notwithstanding—that the symbol originated with the people of Shem from Europe.

of a serpent. The serpent was an emblem of wisdom, and as such appropriately symbolic of the founder of the great Chaldæan nation. In Celtic mythology, Arphaxad says of himself :—

> "I am a Druid,
> I am an Architect,
> I am a Prophet,
> I am a *Serpent.*"

Arphaxad is understood by the Welsh as Aedd-Mawr, father of *Prydian*, supposed by some, instead Brute, to have been the origin of the name Britain.

It is not unusual to hear very learned people refer to the serpent as a Chaldæan *sign*, and then dismiss the idea of it from their minds, little thinking how deeply interesting the investigation of the " *Chaldæan sign* " would prove, if they sought to view it by the light of Bardic tradition, and the researches of recent archæologists. The serpent was not only a Chaldæan but an Israelitish sign, preserved by them even down to the time of Hezekiah. The old form of the word Europe, *Aur-Ab*, signifies a serpent.

If, as it is generally admitted, this was a Chaldæan emblem, who was it emblematic of but Arphaxad (the eldest son of Shem), the light and leader of the

II

Chaldæans? Arphaxad was worshipped as a god, under the form of a serpent, and everywhere throughout Europe, and into Asia, and Egypt, the serpent is to be found cut upon stone, and the principal feature in varieties of ornamental forms.*

Ireland above other places in the world is distinguished by the remains of the serpent in ornamental forms, conspicuous on gold and silver vessels, war instruments, on MSS., and in stone. In Scotland also this serpent form is found upon her stones, bronze armlets, &c., proving how general, and at the same time, mysterious, must have been the serpent among the aboriginal inhabitants of Hibernia and Albion. Among the Scytho-Europeans, the Scandinavians, the Greeks,—whose Red Dragon, "Dragon of the Greeks," according to Pausanias, "was only a large snake,"†—the people that formed the Roman States, indeed, it may be said, among all people, the serpent was a mysterious sign. And so its worship

---

* The serpent-shaped mound of Loch Nell, at the village of Ach-na-Goul, near Inverary, Argyleshire, opened last year by Mr. Skene, F.R.S.S., at the request of the Marquis of Lorne, is an example of the *Serpent of the North*—symbolising, if not Aedd-Mawr, one of his race. Argyle seems to have been especially marked as the abode of serpent worship.

† Pausanias, lib. ii. Corinthiaca, cap. 28, p. 175.

was the first form of idolatry in Europe after Arphaxad.

The pastoral staff or crook (as distinguished from the crozier, which is more correctly in the form of a cross) perhaps owes its origin to the serpent. There was in Dr. Petrie's collection a pastoral staff—found in the last century at Cashel: its handle form is that of a scaled serpent turning round like a volute, with figures introduced in the centre, and on the top part of the staff handle the figure of a fish. The pastoral staff used by the bishops of some Christian Churches is to be traced to the Roman augur; then to the Etrurians, then to the Babylonians, who had it from Asshur, the son of Shem, who with Nimrod and Elam went from Shinar to build Nineveh and its cities. The distinguished descendants of Shem are represented with this crook, as may be seen by any visitor to the Egyptian and Assyrian Courts of the British Museum.*

Notices of the serpent, or " adder," are to be found throughout Celtic mythology. The Legends of Cumberland refer to the *great worm*—no doubt the serpent

---

* The statues of Asshur, Izar-Pal, and many other statues in these Courts bear the crook, in generally the right hand.

is meant. But we must not forget to notice here what is probably the greatest of all relics of serpent symbolism—we allude to the *serpentine* disposition of the 4000 stones of Carnac in Brittany.   ·

Carnac is supposed to mean the *Cairn*, or grave, of *Ac*, sometimes used for the word serpent; or it may mean from the quantity of huge stones resembling a town—the town or city of *Ac* or the serpent, from *Cathair* (pronounced *Căr*), a town or city.

Carnac is the most remarkable place in Armorica, another name for Brittany, and has, perhaps, more extensive druidical remains than are to be found in any one place.   Brittany is a land of Prydian, or Britain, as the word is given in English out of the Welsh. Prydian was known to the Welsh as the son of *Aedd-Mawr*—the Irish is *Ar-Mor*—from whom Armorica took its name.   This patriarchal personage is known also to the Scotch, Irish, and Welsh, as *Arthur*.*   But he seems to have been better known as the Great-Ar (*Ar-Mor*).   The word *Mawr* in Welsh seems to have been substituted for *Parchedig*, literally *Arphaxad.*

---

* Arthur, so often mentioned in Celtic legends, *Art* (for *Ard*), high, and *Ur*, fire, has evident reference to the Chaldæan worship practised by the early Druids, and commemorated in many wonderful and striking fancies by their descendants.

The Arphaxad in the same Celtic dialect means the honourable or great; and in the Gaelic expresses *supreme power*.

Josephus says (cap. vi. s. 4, bk. i.) :—"Arphaxad named the Arphaxadites, who are now called the .Chaldæans." The Culdees, as we will show, were descended from them. The *Ad* of the Koran, who is associated with the people of Noah and of Thamud, and of Abraham, and of the inhabitants of Madian, one of the "cities which were overthrown," was evidently Arphaxad.

Pight, Picti, Pict, are derived from *Phaxad*, or are other forms of the word. The prefix supplied, and we have the Arphaxad of Genesis and Josephus. Therefore the *Picti* (apart from the old notion of *the painted people* of the early history of Scotland) means a people of power, honour, and greatness. Arphaxad then was the first " Druid," " Architect," " Prophet," and " Serpent " of tradition and history.

There could be nothing more suggestive of the countries of the Celt, especially Ireland, than these attributes of Arphaxad. The mind dwells upon the Druid and his mysterious but grand worship; it turns to the knowledge of the Celtic architectural wonders distributed over Ireland, Scotland, England, Wales, and France, conceives that the main business of the Druid was to augur, prophesy, and interpret omens, and to preserve, as was the case, more especially in Ireland, veneration of the serpent.

When St. Patrick is said to have banished the snakes out of Ireland, it may be understood as a figurative way of expressing that he abolished serpent worship. Yet it is curious to observe how the remains of the serpent *form* lingered in the minds of the cloistered monks who have given us such un-paralleled specimens of ornamental initial letters as are preserved in the books of Kells, Ballymote, &c.

Lud, Arphaxad, and Aram would seem to have been neighbours as well as brothers, as appears from the " Altars of Lud;" Lud was nearly the old name of Normandy, adjacent to Armorica.

The names derived from Lud are principally found in Scotland and Wales,* although others are to be found throughout Europe, such as Lugdunum (the ancient Batavorum), now called Leyden.

The Trojāni Ludi, games celebrated in the Roman Circus, and said to have been instituted by Æneas,

* See *ante*, p. 47.

are, it is remarkable, remembered in Wales at the present day. The children there play at " The game of Troy;" and it is the opinion of many lettered Welshmen that the site of the Siege of Troy is to be found in Britain. Annyn-Dro, of the race of *Prydain*, is identified by them as Æneas. There are, perhaps, more wonderful things in connection with the story of Troy to be found in Welsh tradition, than can be summoned out of the Greek and Roman classics.

The name of Aram, the last son of Shem, is apparently prefixed to the word Arimaspian, another title of the Hyperborean, as already noticed.*

The Arimespians, known to Pliny, people dwelling near the rivers of the tribe of Aram, mixed with those called Hyperboreans, descendants of Arphaxad, they were also dwellers in Padan-Aram (sometimes understood as a part of Aram-Naharam, and at other times as the entire of it), or Chaldæa.

---

* Pliny speaks of a river Arimaspias as of Scythia, with golden sands. He talks of the neighbouring people as one-eyed—the eye in the centre of their foreheads (Cyclops), waging continual war against the Griffins, monstrous animals that collect the gold of the rivers—(vii. c. 2.) Arimpheiæi, a people of Scythia, near the Riphian mountains, are also alluded to by Pliny—(vi. c. 7.)

Josephus says Uz, one of the sons of Aram, founded Trachonitis and Damascus.

He spells Hul, '*Ul.*' This person, he tells us, founded Armenia. The name is preserved in the words *Ul*ster, *Ul*swater, and *Hull.*

Of the third son of Aram, Gether, we know little beyond what Josephus informs :—" He founded the Bactrians."[1] If so, their country lays claim to as ancient a prosperity as any probably in Asia. Bactria was the first *entrepot* of trade that we hear of there, and is distinguished for having been the seat of the religion of Zoroaster—magic, astrology, and fire worship, so characteristic of the Chaldæans, and original Irish.

The Jewish historian further makes us aware that Mash, the next son of Aram, was Mesa, and says he " founded the Mesinians ; " now called " Charax Spasini."

We next turn more particularly to the sons of Arphaxad, having devoted considerable space to his brothers and their children.

CHAPTER XII.

SALA.

SALA, Salah, Shelah, or Saleh, different spellings of the name, according to, respectively, Luke iii. 35; Gen. xi. 12; Chron. i. 18; and the Koran, cap. vii. p. 124, *etc.*

As the son of Arphaxad, Sala has left considerable marks of his existence in Europe. One of the oldest druidical seats in Britain is *Cær-Salug*, now called Salesbury, retaining the name of *Sala* in both these forms. The latter form of the word is almost pre-served as applied to the crags near Arthur Seat, Edinburgh, "Salisbury Crags." *

The records of Ban-Chors, or places of meeting for the *white-robed singers* or *priests*, as preserved in the Welsh, point to Salisbury as one of the most important

---

* It requires no stretch of imagination to perceive that Sala, the son of Arphaxad, or, as the Welsh call him, Aedd-Mawr, or *Arthur* in English, would be remembered by his people and honoured in a locality in which he moved, or which was retained by them—so may have " *Arthur Seat*" been first named.

of the druidical *circles*. The next most remarkable *circle* is Cær-Evrog (*Hebrog*), Eboricum, the old name of York, the city of Heber, as it was known from, no doubt, a Heber descended of Sala.

It is rather a remarkable fact that almost always are built on the sites of the old *Cærs*, or seats of the Druids, the cathedrals of modern times, such as Salisbury, York, Canterbury, Winchester, Gloucester, Carlisle, Manchester, Worcester, Chester, Warwick, Lincoln, Chichester, and many others. The seats of the three Arch-Druids were, as before referred to, *Lud*, or London, *Evrog*, or York, and *Cær-Leon*, in Monmouthshire.

One of the descendants of Heber was Levi. Levi, or Lewis, is a Celtic word. Jacob names one of his sons Levi. This word Levi, or Lewis, is in Gaelic *Leubh*.* Its Semetic meaning is generally understood to be *Reader*, or *Priest*.

The name is more frequently known as Lewis, and is in use among the Freemasons of the present day; their Order having preserved much of the Arphaxadite teaching. The eldest son of a "Mason" is called a Lewis.

---

* In Irish *leabher* is a book.

Many families in Europe bear names distinctly pointing to a Levite origin—Lewis, Louis, Levi, Levison, etc., and are more especially peculiar to England. The island of Lewis in the Hebrides, Lewes in Sussex, Lewisham, near London, are places that prove in their names their Celto-Heberian origin. The name *Leubhadh* (Gaelic) points to the Levites of the Mosaic dispensation, reminding . us of the architects whose first-born sons were dedicated to the service of the Temple.

The early "*holy circle*" of men of the Echdradth, or Druids of the unhewn stone-altars, were singers, or men of the *chors*,* singers, reciters, or readers. The word Levite expresses this. The custom of consecrating the first-born son of each family of the Chaldæans to God was preserved by the Jews, and can be traced to have originated with the early Druids. The great priesthood of Arphaxad, and the early teachings of this body, consisted of the right keeping of the records of the Chaldæan rule. The uninitiated can perceive alone from the outward forms and symbols of Freemasonry, that there is

* Choristers.

much in it that originated with the Chaldæan mysteries, and teachings of the Druids.

The three rays of light, symbolising the name of the Most High God, formed thus /||\ ; and the Circle, the Ark, the Temple, the Sun, the Moon, and Stars; the signs of the Zodiac; reference to the "Mariners of the Ark," and their first Grand Master, who was followed by sons of "May," Templars, Knights of St. John (*Oanes*), and the Grand Cross, refer directly to the religion of Noah and his sons. The "Mason" of to-day is instructed in the forms and rites and mysteries of the *diviners* and druids. The diviners and druids of the past have bequeathed to the present much that is to be learned by *the educated.*

Eborecum, one of the grand seats of the Chaldæan faith, and then chief city of Britain, was the centre of Chaldæan power; and Hebrews have held possession there from the most ancient times, as is well known.

That the Chaldæan Hebrews were joined by numbers of the "Children of Israel," and the identity of the "Old House" was lost in that way there is no doubt; neither should we have any hesitation in say-

ing that the Chaldee, or *Culdee*, held the faith of the
Hebrew pure for many ages before, and until some
time after the establishment of Christianity. Those
who held the old faith of the Essinians, accepted
Jesus of Nazareth as a prophet and mediator, and
did so still holding the Hebrew observances of *times*,
sabbaths, and *ancient seasons;* which are proven by
the Calendars of " Feasts and Fasts."

The ancient Jewish customs, as known to us, cor-
roborate what is asserted; that the old Celts * were
no other than Chaldæan, and consequently the
Fathers of Israel. The old Cornish contains as much,
or more, Hebrew than the Welsh.

The wording of a *release* given in the time of one.
of the Henrys, and which is signed by *Jochai* of Kent,
and *Jorin*, his brother Jew, of York, says :—" We,
the undersigned, declare that the prior and the convent of Durham are released from us and from our
heirs, and from all Jews after us from the creation
of the world to the feast of Piers and Paul." The

---

* The reader will remember that the word Celt, although it
did not originate with the people designated under it, (it is .
purely a Greek importation,) is yet employed throughout these
pages to include various branches of the same race : such as
Irish, Welsh, Gaelic, Armoric, etc.

tenure of these men of York, in their own eyes, must have been a most ancient one. The above is taken from a *Starra*, or Jewish covenant of Durham, which was noticed in the *Jewish Chronicle* some time about July of last year. It is only one of many such like deeds that go to prove the "ancient people of God" to have been long holders of property in England. The persecution and shameful manner of defrauding, banishing, and preventing them from retaining their ancient land-holdings are matters that disgrace many pages of English history.

The death-bed of William the Conqueror was not the only one haunted by remembrances of cruelty and injustice done to the House of Israel. He only followed the steps of the Romans, who had for centuries striven to extirpate the Druids, and Priests and Levites who crowded the Banchors, and filled the "cities of the Harpers of the Hyper-boreans."

It was one thing to change the names of the places, and try to Latinise and alter everything, but the hearts of the Celtic people could not be changed. The bards, *coarbs*, and druids kept their faith, and handed it down to their children in verses, that have gone

up to the Most High ever since Shinar was first
peopled.

The Psalter of " Old Sarum" (Salisbury) is no new
song ; and Asaph, and Daniel, and David were names
known long before the time the Psalms were collected
by the son of Jesse. The "Laws of Dyvnwal-
Moelmud" are the laws of a Daniel who lived
long anterior to the Chaldæan Prophet who was
delivered from the "lions' den." *Daniel* of Bangor
was founder of a choir of Levites before this Chaldæan Prophet was born.

Sons of the Daniel first mentioned are the Mac
Daniels, Daniels, the MacDonnels, and Dynevalls,
&c. The wars of the MacDonnels and MacLeods
of the Isles, as referred to elsewhere in this work,
were of particular significance, far beyond what is
generally understood of them by the student of
Erse history. The ancient people referred to by the
Venerable Bede, as Culdees, were composed of many
of the above families. This description identifies
them with the Essenians and Therepuetes.

A few more words about Sala. The recurrence of
the name so frequently in the Psalms,* and the

* It is repeated by itself no less than seventy-four times in the
Psalms, and thrice in Habakkuk.

singularity of its position throughout, has puzzled many. It stands separate in the Psalms—

The earth and all the inhabitants thereof are dissolved: I bear up the pillars of it. SELAH. *Ps.* lxxv., 3.

The Arabs of Jocktan took with them numerous legends of Sala to their country (as we know it in the present day, Arabia), and to Europe again with Mahomet.

To the Mahometan the story of Salah is quite familiar. He is represented by them to be of *the land of the ancient Arab,*—this must not be understood as the *dwelling-place,* but *the land from which they first migrated;* that part of *Shinar* called Irem, near, or in which was, Al Ras, Madian—in fact, the land of Ad and Thamud, which means of Arphaxad (Aedd-Mawr), and of Terah, the father of Abraham.

Some places of consequence in Europe yet retain the name of Sala :—Sala, a town of Thrace, near the mouth of the Hebrus; Salamis, or Salamina, a town at the east of Cyprus; Salapia, a town of Apulia, to which Hannibal retired after the battle of Cannæ; Salara, a town of Africa-propria, taken by Scipio; and Salamanca, in Spain.

The Salasci, a people of Cisalpine Gaul, were descended of Sala.*

There are some names of people corresponding to Sala—Sala, Salaman, and, perhaps, Soloman and Sale.

* They were in continual war with the Romans, and at one time cut off over 10,000 of them under Appius Cladius.

114

CHAPTER XIII.

HEBER.

THE Irish records and traditions agree that Heber came from Iberia, and that the south of Ireland was his portion : *

> " Heber took the south of Eri,
> The order was so agreed on
> With its activity, with its power,
> With its harmony.
> With its victims, with its grandeur,
> With its hospitality ;
> With its vivacity combined with hardiness—
> With its loveliness, with its purity."

So Nennius gives it. Heber is described as a "crowned-horseman." This Heber, or another one of the name, was the precursor of tribes of Arads or Arabs (the *d* is used for *b* in many of the old Irish MSS., as well as in modern Irish books). Nennius (p. 257) speaks of *Corpre Arad; Ared Tire, Arad Chlhach*. Again, in the same book, these tribes are

* Some believe that Heber occupied the *north* of Ireland.

called *Cairphi Arad, Arad Thiri, Arad Cliach.*
O'Donovan describes them as the tribes settled in
Du-harra, in Tipperary. Nennius (p. 569) says the
descendants of Eber are *Eoghanachts* in every place :

> At Ani-Loch Line, Cassel, Glendamerin, and Ros-Argaid ;
> Eochaidh of Rathlinn without oppression,
> Magnificent their apparel.

In the days of the sons of Heber, Jocktan, and
Peleg, there was a division of the earth—that is to
say, countries were apportioned them. Peleg is
believed by some to be *Pelasgus*, and, therefore, that
Greece was settled in by his people. Peleg is in the
Bible sometimes called Phalec.*

Jocktan took a tribe into Arabia. The "Arab
al Ariba," the *genuine* Arab, claims to be a son
of Jocktan, the son of Heber. He prides himself
upon being of purer blood than the Ishmaelite
Arab. To the Arabs generally Heber is known as
Hud, and they narrate many Celtic traditions and
superstitions. We give a few of them. There was in
Old Gaul a common belief among the people, that if
witches tied knots in a cord and breathed upon them,

---

* There are legends of *Paluc* in the Manx Island.

uttering at the same time words of mystery, they would reduce the mind and body of the person they wished to injure. In France in the present day there is a relic of this superstition called *Nouër l'eguellette.** It is referred to in the Koran (cap. CXIII). "IN THE NAME OF THE MOST MERCIFUL GOD. Say, I fly for refuge unto the Lord of the day-break, that he may deliver me from the mischief of those things which he hath created, and from the mischief of the night when it cometh on, *and from the mischief of women blowing on knots.*"† . . . . The followers of "The Prophet" (according to *Savary*) "have an · implicit faith in the words contained in these two

---

* It is similar to what is attributed to the Norse wizards when they *sell mariners a wind.*

† We take the following from Sale's Koran as an illustration of this strange practice:

"The commentators relate that Lobeid, a Jew, with the assistance of his daughters, bewitched Mohammed by tying eleven knots on a cord, which they hid in a well; whereupon Mohammed falling ill, God revealed this chapter and the following: And Gabriel acquainted him with the use he was to make of them, and of the place where the cord was hidden, accord-ing to whose directions the prophet sent Ali to fetch the cord, and the same being brought, he repeated the two chapters over it, and at every verse (for they consist of eleven) a knot was loosed, till, on finishing the last words, he was entirely freed from the charm."—Note, p. 505.

chapters (caps. CXIII. and CXIV). They consider them as a sovereign specific against magic, lunar influences, and the temptations of the evil spirit. They never fail to repeat them evening and morning." There is another Arabic tradition reflecting upon an Irish one. It is about the birds of *Ross-Dela*, in the Koran *Al Rass.* We give Mr. Sale's note upon it :

"The commentators are at a loss where to place Al Rass. According to one opinion, it was the name of a well (as the word signifies) near Midian, about which some idolators having fixed their habitations, the prophet Shoaib was sent to preach to them ; but they not believing on him, the well fell in, and they and their houses were all swallowed up. Another supposes it to have been a town Yamâma, where a remnant of the Thamudites settled, to whom a prophet was also sent, but they slaying him, were utterly destroyed. Another thinks it was a well near Antioch, where Habib al Najjar (whose tomb is still to be seen there, being frequently visited by the Mohammedans) was martyred. And a fourth takes Al Rass to be a well in Hadramant, by which dwelt some idolatrous Thamudites, whose prophet was Handha, or Khantala (for I find the name written both ways) Ebn Safwân. These people were first annoyed by certain monstrous birds, called Ankâ, which lodged in the mountain above them, and used to snatch away their children, when they wanted other prey : but this calamity was so far from humbling them, that on their prophet's calling down a judgment upon them, they killed him, and were all destroyed."—(Koran, cap. xxv., entitled Al Forkan,* revealed at Mecca.)

Now let us see how the Irish tale resembles this, then we will conclude that inasmuch as the commentators could not find Al Rass in the East, it is beyond any doubt the Ross Dela of Ireland.

From the Irish version of Nennius, published by the Irish Archæological Society, we take the following account, in connection with Ross Dela, of one of the wonders † of Eri ; it is, according to the book of " Leinster," or " Glen-da-locha " :—

* *Forkan* is one of the names for the Koran.

† The *Wonders* are fully treated of in a tract to be found in the MSS. Library of Trinity College, Dublin. The *Mirabilia Hibernia* are described beside Nennius, by Geraldus Cambrensis Ralf Higden, in his " Polychronicon," nearly copied from Geraldus ; and by Ware, in his " Antiquities of Ireland," by Harris.

" A belfry of fire which was seen at Ross Dela, during the space of nine hours, and blackbirds without number, coming out and going into it. One great bird *was* among them, and the smaller birds used to nestle in his feathers when they went into the belfry. And they all came out together. And they took up dogs with them in their talons, and they let them drop down to earth and they died. The birds flew away from the place afterwards, and the wood upon which they perched bent under them to the ground. And the oak upon which the said great bird perched, was carried by him by the roots out of the earth, and where they went to is not known." Ross-Dela, the place where the miraculous tower of fire was seen, is very little altered in name—it is now *Ross-dalla,** a townland in the parish of Durrow, near Kilbiggan, county of Westmeath. The Four Masters, in the year 1054, describe the phenomenon : " A belfry of fire was seen in the air, over Ross-deala, on the Sunday of the feast of St. Guirgi (George) for five hours ; blackbirds innumerable *passing* into and out of it, and one large bird in the middle of them,

* The name Ross is applied to a great many places in Ireland ; it is peculiar to that country and Scotland.

and the little birds went under his wings when they went into the belfry."

About twenty times the saying :—"*Remember Ad, and Thamud, and those who dwelt at Al-Rass*"—is repeated in the Koran.* The "Wood near *Madian;*" the cities and lofty castles that were overthrown, and many other particular allusions, in the same book, point to Ireland as the country in which was Al-Rass. We will leave it to the reader to decide for himself whether it was in Ireland. It is to our mind impossible to disbelieve the Semetic affinity of the early Celt, which the above goes to prove.

It is beyond question that the Arab knows Heber as Hud, and worthy of notice that the country of Eboricum, Yorkshire, is thought to have taken this latter name from Jocktan. There is a Yäûk mentioned in the Koran, and by some believed to be no other

---

* There is another phrase found in cap. L.,—"The people of Noah and those who dwelt at Al-Rass, and Thamud, and Ad, and Pharaoh, accuse the prophets of imposture before the Meccans, and also the brethren of Lot, and the inhabitants of the wood, near Midian, and the people of Tobba." It is curious to mark the signification of this last word : in Irish it means *well*, and, than Ireland, no country in the world is more characterised by *wells*, and no people have more claim to be called the " people of Tobba " than the Irish.

than Jocktan, the leader of the Arab-al-Arab. We have said another name of Heber was Hud. This name remains plentifully enough in the British Islands, especially in Yorkshire,—Hudswell, Huddersfield, Hudnel, Huddington, Huddleston, are places all in Yorkshire; and the family name Hudson is not only found there by the hundred, but in most parts of England. There are many also of the name of Huddleston. In the Irish Calendar of Saints there is a *Mochudee,** which appears to have a kindred resemblance to the original Hud. There is beside, a *Machod* (Latinized Mauchguid), referred to in the Additional Notes to the Irish Nennius, p. iii.; but the explanation of it is peculiar: "Manchester in Warwickshire? or Manchester?"

In the Irish legendary accounts of Heber there is much that may be regarded as genuine history. A great deal of Keating's "History of Ireland" remains indisputably true, while other parts of it may be questioned, and some things altogether disbelieved. But, although we have not endeavoured to shew much to prove the identity of the Heber of Genesis and the Irish Heber, still we cannot but think that it is quite *possible* they may have been the same person. Some accounts state

---

* *Mahody* seems to have been also a divinity of Eliphanta.

that the Irish Heber is said to have reigned B.C. 2737, while other about 1000 years before; and the Heber of Genesis somewhere near B.C. 2260; at any rate, we are told that his son Peleg was born in 2247 B.C., when his father was thirty-four years of age.

In 1883 before the Christian era, the Pelasgi are said to have entered the Peloponessus and inhabited Argolis. It has been argued of late, and with some show of reason, that Peleg settled in Greece, and that he was no other than Pelasgus. It is a strange fact that some Irish accounts say the Grecians were called in the *old* Irish *Gaoidheal—Gael.* We have not ourselves seen this anywhere but in Keating, but if it is true, it goes to strengthen our opinion that the Greeks and their tongue were descended from the Gaelic* family and language of Heber.

After talking of the attempt of Nimrod to erect the tower of Babel, and the consequent confusion

---

* Keating says—"The family of Cecrops, according to St. Austin, began about the time that Jacob was born, about 432 years after the Deluge. Hector Bœtius, in his 'History of Scotland,' says—that the Gadelians were in Egypt when Moses was working wonders in that country for the delivery of the Israelites, and the book of the Irish Invasion agree with that computation," (p. 3).

of speech, Keating says—" But the wisdom of God
thought fit to preserve the genuine and original language, which was the Hebrew, in the family of Heber
from whom it was called the Hebrew tongue." And
for opposing the designs of Nimrod he furthermore
relates—" The faithful Heber for his piety was
rewarded with a continuance of the original speech
in his own family, who preserved it uncorrupt, and
in its native purity delivered it to posterity," p. 59.

Bearing in mind the comparatively small period of
time between the two Hebers (according to one of
the citations already quoted), and that the difference
may be accounted for by inexactness of the chroniclers
of the Druid and the Jew, there is not much to
decide us against believing that both Hebers are
identical.

" The land of Heber and the Hebrew "—where
is it, if not in Western Europe? The Hebrews of
course had possessions in the East, but the signs of
them remaining there are few, indeed, as compared to
those appealing to us for recognition in the West of
the two Continents.

DESCENDANTS OF HEBER.

Of Reu, Serug, and Nahor, descendants of Heber, there are, as far as we know, few traces in Europe. Reu is referred to in the Irish Nennius :—

"*Sru*, son of Es-Ru, went afterwards ;" *e. g.*, as we take it, Serug went from his country after the departure—whither we cannot tell—of Rue, his father. But of Serug, we are told he went

> Round by the gloomy north rapidly to *Shire-Riffi*.
> He settled in fiery Golgather.
> A noble deed,
> There dwelt his descendants without disgrace
> Two hundred years.

We presume they went northwards, and over Scandinavia. Nahor, the father of Tera, remained in Ur of the Chaldees, if we judge by the city called after, and supposed to have been built by him. Aram-*Nahar*am, one of the names of Chaldæa and Mesopotamia, seems to retain the name.

CHAPTER XIV.

TERAH AND ABRAM.

TERAH, son of Nahor, spelt in the first book of
the Bible as above, and in Luke as Thara.
Zarah, as we find it in the Talmud, is the name
of the father of Abram. The Koran points to
his people as the Thamudites. Other names for
him are, by the Persians and Mahommedans, *Azer*,
and *Athar*, in Eusebius. Some of the Rabbins say
Terah was priest, and chief of the order. "Abram,
his son, was rich, and had much silver and gold,
men-servants, and maid-servants, and was a prince
when he reached Damascus," *Thamud*, the name
given to Terah by the ancient Arabs, is unquestionably applied to no other place than *Thomond*, one
of the ancient kingdoms of Ireland, known by that
name up to the reign of Henry VIII., when it was
changed into Clare county. Terah's name in the
present day, is recognisable as the place as well as
the name—Tara!

Besides Tara, there are, in the same quarter, names

of import to Bible commentators, but which are supposed by them to be for ever enveloped in Eastern
fog. These names are Teman, Teman's town, Midian,
and Cushan.

Tara, by Latin and English writers, is named
Temoria and Temor. *Mur*, in Irish, signifies
"mound," and *Tea*, according to Amergin, was a
queen of Heremon, brother of Heber. Hence
Temoria and *Temor*. There were national conventions held there, and of great celebrity. They were
called *Feis Tamhrach*. There were in Meath four
royal palaces, at Temoria or Tara, at Tailten, at
Tlachtga, and at Uisneach. It is said that *Taillte*,
queen of *Eochaidh*, son of Eirc, who was the last
king of the Firbolgs buried there, gave her name
to Tailten. It was a place of much importance, for
great assemblies of the people were held there annually
in August, at which recreations and sports, nearly
the same as the Olympic games of Greece, were
exhibited, marriage contracts ratified, &c. Teltown,
between Killo and Navan, near the river Black-
water, is the modern name and place of Tailten.
Tlachtga, another place of the palaces of the old
monarchs, according to the "Four Masters," was

situated near Athboy, and was celebrated as a seat of Druidism. The hill of *Uisneach*—the name of the place of the fourth-mentioned palace—in the barony of Rathconrath, in Westmeath, between Mullingar and Athlone, was another noted seat of Druidism.

Temhair-na-Riogh, or Tara of the kings, was the chief seat of the *Ard Righ*, the high king or monarch who presided over Meath and the five provincial kings. Meath, Ulster, Connaught, Leinster, and Munster, formed the Irish Pentarchy. The Firbolg, Tuath de Danan, and Milesian kings resided chiefly at Tara. Cormac, monarch of Ireland in the third century, had one of the greatest palaces at Tara. An account of it is given by various writers; one of the best is by Owen Connellan. As it cannot fail to interest our readers, this is it :—

" Cormac's palace at Tara . . . . was called Teach *Miodhchuarta*, signifying either the house of banquets, or the house of conventions ; also *Teach-na-Laech*, which meant the House of the Heroes ; and it was the place in which were held the great *Feis Teamhrach*, or conventions of Tara, ... and in its halls the monarchs gave their great banquets,

and entertained the provincial kings, princes, and
chiefs. It is stated that the length of the structure
was 300 feet, the breadth 50 cubits or about 80 feet,
and the height 30 cubits or nearly 50 feet; it contained numerous apartments beside the royal bed-
chamber, and had on it fourteen doors. And it is
stated that there were seven other great habitations
adjoining the palace. Cormac was the son of Art,
son of Con of the Hundred Battles, monarch of
Ireland of the race of Heremon, and he was one of
the most celebrated of the Irish kings for munificence,
learning, wisdom, and valour; and the glories of his
palace at Tara were for many ages the theme of the
Irish bards. Amongst other splendid articles, it is
mentioned that he had at the royal banquets one
hundred and fifty massive goblets of pure gold.
Cormac's palace was situated on the hill of Tara, and
a great part of the circular earthen ramparts, together
with a large mound in the centre, still remain. The
palace is considered to have been built chiefly of wood
from the oak forests, in ancient times so abundant in
Ireland, and was probably in part formed of stone work,
or a fortress of Cyclopean architecture, composed of
great stones without cement; and though few of the

stones now remain, they may have been removed in
the course of ages, and placed in other buildings, particularly as the hill of Tara was easily accessible ;
and though this palace could not be compared with
the more elegant buildings of more modern times,
yet it was distinguished for all the rude magnificence
peculiar to those earlier ages. On the hill of Tara
were erected several other ráths or mounds and
fortresses, as mentioned by several ancient historians,
amongst others *Cathair Crofinn*, that is, the fortress,
city, or seat of Crofinn, so called from Crofinn, one öf
the *Tuath-de-Danaan* queens ; and this building was
also named *Tur-Trean-Teamhrach*, signifying the
strong tower of Tara ; and as the term Cathair was
applied only to stone buildings, this was probably
a fortress of Cyclopean architecture, the stones of
which may have been removed in course of time ;
and the Danans are stated by old writers to have
built fortresses in other parts of Ireland, particularly
that called *Aileach Neid*, in Tyrconnell, situated on a
great hill near Lough Swilly, in Donegal, and of this
Cyclopean fortress some ruins still remain. At Tara
was also the building called *Mur Ollamham*, or the
house of the learned, in which resided the bards,

K

brehons, and other learned men, and likewise *Rath-na-Seanadh*, which signifies either the fort of the convention, or of the synods, and said to be so called from great meetings held there at different times by St. Patrick, St. Adamnan, St. Brenden, and St. Ruadhan ; also *Rath-na-Riogh*, or the fortress of the kings, *Dumha-na-nGiall*, or the mound of the hostages, where there was a fortress in which the hostages were kept ; and *Dumha-na-nBan-amus*, signifying the mound of the warlike women, which was probably a habitation or a burial place of those ancient heroines ; there was likewise a habitation called Cluan-Feart, or the Sacred Retreat, which was the residence of the Vestal Virgins or Druidesses, according to Dr. O'Connor and others. At Tara were also habitations for the warriors, Druids, Brehons, and bards, and also for the provincial kings, princes, and chiefs, who attended at the great national conventions, and therefore the place was considered as a city in those ancient times. There are many remains of the mounds, raths, and other antiquities still at Tara, but many of those mounds and raths have been levelled in the course of ages. According to the ancient histories many of the kings, queens,

and warriors of the early ages were buried at Tara,
and several sepulchral mounds were raised there to
their memory. In one of the earthen ramparts at
Tara were discovered, in the year 1810, two of the
ornaments called *torques*, a sort of golden collar of
spiral or twisted workmanship, and of a circular form,
open at one side, worn on the necks of the ancient
kings and chiefs, and similar to those worn by the
ancient kings and chiefs of Gaul, and were called
torc in the Celtic language. One of the torques
discovered at Tara is five feet seven inches in length,
and something more than twenty-seven ounces in
weight, and all formed of the purest gold; the other
torque is beyond twelve ounces in weight, and they
form some of the most interesting remains of ancient
Irish art."

Many poets have written of ancient Tara, the best
of them are Amergin, chief bard of Dermot, monarch
of Ireland in the sixth century; Cuan O'Lochain,
a celebrated bard who died in A.D. 1024; and
Keneth O'Hartigan, of the tenth century, whose
poem is contained in the "Book of Ballymote,"
—here is the English of a few of his beautiful
verses :—

O world of deceitful beauty,
The agreeable drinking feast of a hundred heroes ;
False are its attractions, numerous to mention,
Except the adoration of the King of all.

Every law recorded has passed away,
Every right under the sun has been destroyed,
And Temor to-day though a wilderness,
Was once the meeting-place of heroes.

Fair was its many-sided tower,
Where assembled heroes famed in story,
Many were the tribes to which it was inheritance,
Though to-day but a green grassy land.

It was a famous fortress of wisdom ;
It was ennobled with warlike chiefs,
To be viewed it was a splendid hill
During the time of Cormac O'Cuinn.

When Cormac was in his grandeur
Brilliant and conspicuous was his course,
No fortress was found equal to Temor,
It was the secret of the road of life.

Strong was the power of hosts
Of that King who obtained Temor ;
It is better for us to record the many tribes
And the numerous families of his household.

Nine ramparts or rough strong trenches,
With nine surrounding mounds,
With groves of fair trees,
And it was a strong and famous fortress.

This great house of a thousand heroes,
With tribes it was delightful,
A fair bright fortress of fine men,
Three hundred feet was its measure.

Its circuit was well arranged,
Nor was it narrow by a faulty construction,
Nor too strong for separate apartments,
Six times five cubits was its height.

A fit habitation for a King of Erin
In which was distributed sparkling wine ;
It was a fortress, a rampart, and a stronghold,
In it were three times fifty condos.

There were in it fifty warriors with swords
Who were the guards of this fortress,
Which truly was a noble residence,
And there were two couches in each apartment.

Grand was the host which attended there,
And their weapons were glittering with gold ;
There were three times fifty splendid apartments,
And each apartment held fifty persons.

Seven cubits of exact measure
Were the dimensions of the fire-place,
Before which the active attendants
Lighted up the brilliant lamps.

There were seven splendid chandeliers of brass,
Of bright and beautiful appearance,
In that fair and sunny palace
Of feasts and ornamental goblets.

Pleasingly brilliant was its light,
And twice seven in numbers were its doors ;
It was a law ordained by the King
That he should first drink to his guests.

And very great were his guests in number,
Three hundred partook of each festive drinking ;
Fifty were learned and noble lawgivers
In company with the exalted upright Prince.

Fifty were festive pleasing companions,
With fifty great and famous heroes,
And fifty warriors standing around
To attend as guards on the warlike king.

Three hundred cup-bearers handed around
Three times fifty splendid goblets
To each of the numerous parties there,
Which cups were of gold or of silver all.

Ornamented with pure and precious stones
Thirty hundred were entertained
By the son of Art on each day.
   *   *   *   *   *

Enlightened was his train of bards,
Who kept their records in careful order,   [each art.
And what they said was respected by the professors in

The household of the hosts let us enumerate
Who were in the house of Temor of the tribes.
This is the exact enumeration—
Fifty above a thousand of warriors.

When Cormac resided at Temor
His fame was heard by all the exalted,
And a king like the son of Art Aenfaer
There came not of the men of the world.

The description of - the Palace of Cormac may
be applied in a general way, more or less, to the
other Palaces of Meath before alluded to, and be
taken to signify that there was great prosperity and
civilization in Ireland long anterior to Cormac's reign,
in the third century, long before the introduction of
Christianity—indeed, a civilization existant before
and with those of Babylon and Nineveh.

Look into English history, and think that, while
the ancient Briton was subjected for three hundred
years to the Romans, from Cæsar's success up to
the time of Cormac's reign, the independence of
Ireland was guaranteed by the numerous and warlike companions-in-arms that assembled periodically
at Tara from every part of the country, over which
were tens of thousands of proud, hardy, and disci-
plined troops, ready and eager at any moment to
raise the banners of their chieftains, to shout their
war-cries and rush to battle.

Not only are we justified in concluding that Ireland was great in arms in pre-Christian times, but

an examination of her code of laws, preserved to us in the Irish language and in an English translation by the Irish Archæological Society, convinces us of the then high cultivation of her Brehons and public men. But such references as have been made to the Gael Abaris by Pythagoras, and by others shortly after him, go a great way to prove that the Greeks and Romans received not only the elements of their religious systems from the Celts, so called, but their jurisprudence, which can be as distinctly traced to a Chaldee-Celtic source as their languages and themselves. Hence it follows, that we can be in no way wrong in assigning to Ireland the rise of Terah and Abram.

Before we endeavour to follow Abram out of Ireland, we will submit the following from Vallancy, which, if only half of it be true, is enough, in our mind, to indicate, at least, the passage of a people eastward from Tara.

Different compounds with the word Tara :—

"*Tamhar*, a tower, the great tower ; *Tamhra*, now Tara, *Arathall*, afar off, far beyond, migration, hence.

"*Taradh*, a ferry-boat.

- " *Taraseach,* from beyond the mountains.

" *Tartaise,* a distant habitation.

" *Tartearach,* transmarine.

" *Taralpach,* transalpine.

" *Tarrus,* a pilgrimage, a journey.

" *Tardala,* migrating tribes ; a tribe of people, together with the religion belonging to that tribe. When our Ari-Coti settled in Celti Lucia, the island of the Coti or Gades, some crossed over to the continent of Spain (? no doubt Africa), and were called Tardela, migrating tribes. And when at Tyre, or in that vicinity, in their traffic to and fro, speaking of Spain, they would naturally say they came from *Tartaise,* the former habitation or home ; hence the *Tarduli* and *Tarlesie* of Spain."

It would be easy for us to give examples of hundreds of places in Europe and Asia, the meanings of which are to be found in the Celtic languages, the Sanscrit, and often in the Hebrew; but we will not wait to do so here, but simply point to this list of names, as signifying the direction taken by a people, from the district of the British Islands, at any rate. through Spain to the south, and then over the north of Africa, making settlements, and to Egypt, Arabia, and Hindostan, and north, through Asia. This, it may be, was the route the forefathers of Terah and Abram took—the Nimrod and Assur of Babylonian and Ninevite history. Whether they migrated in this direction or over Europe, makes little difference, for their location in the East is not to be disputed.

The *Thera*puetes and Essenes are names of a distinguished *sect* of the Hebrews. It was the third sect, little known, but the one that ruled in Chaldæa. The Culdee, according to the Venerable Bede (and he was right) was the same as the Essene.

It is said in Gen. xi., 31, that " Terah took Abram his son, and Lot the son of Haran his son's son, and Sarai his daughter-in-law, his son Abram's wife; and they went forth with them from Ur of the Chaldees, to go into the land of Canaan; and they came unto Haran, and dwelt there."

The *Tardala* and *Tarleise* of Spain were people of Abram. If we view them as such we must believe that Abram crossed from Spain into Africa; so we account for his possession of *camels*, besides

other cattle. And possibly the gold and silver
vessels he is said to have been in possession of
when he sojourned from Egypt into Asia were not
accumulations on the way, but were for the most part
brought with him from Ur of the Chaldees. This
is more likely, as we find that some of the gold and
silver ornaments found in Ireland are as old as any
found elsewhere.

Abram, because he was to be the father of many
nations, is henceforth called Abraham (Gen. xvii. 5);
and in the same chapter, verse 15, Sarai, his wife,
born in Ur, was thought worthy of being called *Sarah*
(שרה), or *princess* :—

"And God said unto Abraham, As for Sarai thy wife, thou
shalt not call her name Sarai, but Sarah shall her name be.
"And I will bless her, and give thee a son also of her : yea, I
will bless her, and she shall be a mother of nations; kings of
people shall be of her."—*Gen.* xvii., 15, 16.

This passage denotes that God designed the greatness of Abram and Sarai—personages that we can by no
means leave out of our notices of the people of Heber.

In the year 1872 B.C., when Abraham was dwelling
at Beersheba, it was told him: "Behold, Milcah, she
hath also borne children unto thy brother Nahor;"
their names were: "Huz his first-born, and Buz his

brother, and Kemuel the father of Aram, and Chesed, and Hazo, and Pildash, and Jidlaph, and Bethuel. And Bethuel begat Rebekah: these eight Milcah did bear to Nahor, 'Abraham's brother" (Gen. xxii. 20–23). Who told Abraham of his brother Nahor's children we do not learn. Whether the news was brought by Midianite *merchantmen*, who are recorded to have gone to and fro between the British Islands and the East, taking tin, and bringing back spices, and carrying news from one distant part to the other; or whether it was a divine revelation at that time, as a special reward of his faith, is not stated; but it was told Abraham just after he had been to offer up Isaac in the land of Moriah. When Sarah was dead, he acted upon this information, and sent for Bethuel's daughter, Rebekah, whose birth-place was the city of Nahor, in Chaldæa. "Abraham was old, and well stricken in age: and the Lord had blessed Abraham in all things." (Gen. xxiv. 1.) Abraham administers an oath to Eleazar of Damascus: "'And I will make thee swear by the Lord, the God of heaven, and the God of the earth, that thou shalt not take a wife unto my son of the daughters of the Canaanites, among whom I dwell: but thou shalt go unto my country, and to my kindred, and take a wife unto my son Isaac.' And the servant said unto him, ' Peradventure the woman will not be willing to follow me unto this land : must I needs bring thy son again unto the land from whence thou camest ? ' And Abraham said unto him, ' Beware thou that thou bring not my son thither again : The Lord God of heaven, which took me from my father's house, and from the land of my kindred, and which spake unto me, and that sware unto me, saying, " Unto thy seed will I give this land ; " he shall send his angel before thee, and thou shalt take a wife unto my son from thence. . . . . . And the servant took ten camels of the camels of his master, and departed, for all the goods of his master were in his hand: and he arose, and went to Mesopotamia,*

* It will be recollected by the reader who has been good enough to follow us up to this point, that Mesopotamia is a descriptive word, signifying "*between two rivers*," or dry land between waters ; consequently, a Mesopotamia may well have been in the west. That there was more than one Mesopotamia may be inferred from what Stephen says :—" The God of Glory appeared to our father Abraham when he was in Mesopotamia, before he dwelt in Charran. *Then came he out of the land of the Chaldæans*, and dwelt in Charran ; and from thence, when his father was dead, he removed him into the land wherein ye now dwell." (*Acts* vii. 2, 3, 4.) And again, in Gen. xv. 7, we have :

unto the city of Nahor." What was the reason that Abraham desired to send to Chaldæa for a daughter of his own house to be the wife of his son Isaac?—that the pure descent of the line should be unbroken. A daughter of the house of Heber was needed to preserve the purity of the patriarchal stock.

It was no small journey in these days from Asia to the west of Europe, but then the guide was an "Angel of the Lord," and the journey, long and difficult as it was with the ten camels, came to an end, for we read that he made his camels kneel down without the city, by a well of water, at the time of the evening, "even the time that women go out to draw water." Eleazar speaks, and prays to the Lord for Isaac and the wife that is to be his. We give the picture of Rebekah as she appears to Eleazar :

"And it came to pass that before he had done speaking, that, behold, Rebekah came out, who was

—" And he said unto him, I am the Lord who brought thee out of *Ur of the Chaldees,* to give thee this land to inherit it." The Ur of the Chaldees and the Mesopotamia spoken of as the first dwelling place of Abraham, and the land of the Chaldæans spoken of in the *Acts,* as above, are manifestly the same place, although far distant from the neighbourhood of Damascus and Jerusalem.

born to Bethuel, son of Milcah, the wife of Nahor, Abraham's brother, with her pitcher upon her shoulder. And the damsel was very fair to look upon, and she went down to the well, and filled her pitcher, and came up. And the servant ran to meet her, and said, Let me, I pray thee, drink a little water of thy pitcher. And she said, Drink, my lord. And she hasted and let down her pitcher upon her hand, and gave him drink. And when she had done giving him drink, she said, I will draw water for thy camels also, until they have done drinking."

The latter part of this quotation opens up a question as to the figures to be found on the stone crosses of Ireland and Scotland, and representing laden camels kneeling and standing to drink. These figures are to be seen in the caves, and delineated upon the stone monuments of both countries, with a fidelity that proves the sculptors to have been perfectly acquainted with these, to us now, travellers only of the Eastern deserts.

We cannot tell whether these camel sculptures are intended to represent . the visit of Eleazar and his attendants, or whether it was possible then for them to have reached the district of the British Islands as

an integral portion of the Continent; but certain
it is that if these islands became, through earthquake,
disintegrated from the Continent, the occurence must
have been after Eleazar's journey, that is, in 789 B.C.,
if we are to believe the only references to such having
happened—those of Amos, Ezekiel, and Habakkuk.*

"And it came to pass as the camels had done
drinking, that the man took a golden ear-ring, of half
a shekel weight, and two bracelets for her hands, of
ten shekels weight of gold, and said : whose daughter
art thou ?—tell me, I pray thee, is there room in thy
father's house for us to lodge in.   And she said unto
him : I am the daughter of Bethuel son of Milcah.
. . . . We have both straw and provender, and
room to lodge in : And the man bowed down his ·
head and worshipped the Lord : And Rebekah had a
brother and his name was Laban, and Laban ran out
unto the man unto the well, and it came to pass when
he saw the ear-ring and bracelets upon his sister's
hands, and when he heard the words of Rebekah his
sister . . . . he welcomed him, and he said
'Come in, thou blessed of the Lord.'"   Laban, her
brother, encouraged the traveller, and the message

* Hab. iii. ; Ezek. xxxviii. 19, 20 ; Amos i. 1.

from Abraham, and the rich jewels found favour with the maiden. And "I will go," said Rebekah, in reply to "Wilt thou go with this man?" And they sent away Rebekah their sister and her nurse, and Abraham's servant with his men, and they blessed Rebekah, and said unto her : "Thou art our sister; *be thou the mother of thousands of millions.*"

The chapter (Gen. xxiv. 63, &c.) closes with reference to her reception by Isaac : "As he went to meditate in the field at even-tide, he lifted up his eyes and saw, and behold, the camels were coming" —with the fair Hebrew girl who was to occupy Sarah's tent, and become one of the mothers of Israel.

Isaac, then, has satisfied his father's wish, and taken a wife out of Chaldæa ; the race of Heber was thus preserved in its purity. Abraham sent to his father's country for a wife for his son, and we may take it from this that there was more than love of country in it—that there was a civilization and prosperity in Europe before the time of Abraham; that, indeed, Europe was the *Shinar*, or the "*Old Land*," that has so bewildered Bible students.

Terah seems to have left in these islands, particularly Ireland, more satisfactory indications of his dwelling and name than are to be found for Abraham, notwithstanding he stands out in far bolder relief than Terah, which is to be accounted for by the careful registration of his greatness by his people in the East, and who, save noticing Terah in their genealogies, have little to say of him except what is to be found in Joshua xxiv. 2, 3, 4. He is speaking to the elders of Israel : " Thus saith the Lord God of Israel, Your fathers dwelt on the other side of the Flood in old times, even *Terah*, the father of Abraham, and the father of Nachor, and they served other gods ; and I took your father Abraham from the other side of the Flood, and led him throughout all the land of Canaan, and multiplied his seed, and gave him Isaac; and I gave unto Isaac Jacob and Esau, and I gave unto Esau Mount Seir, to possess it; but Jacob and his children went down into Egypt."

The Koran, cap. vi., p. 105, refers to Terah. It throws great light, if we are to believe it, upon the origin of the *Teraphim*—family gods, or household images similar to the *Penates* of the Romans.

We have noticed before that the *Tardala* and *Tar-*

leise were descended of Terah. They were a travelling or migrating tribe, and must have assisted greatly to spread abroad the religion of the Therapuetes, else it is possible we would have no records to show to us its similarity, indeed identity, with the faith of Abraham and of the ancient Druids.

In the Welsh language Abraham is known as *Avruey*, "the contemplative," and his name lives in connection with the Abred of the Druids. The great monument of *Abri*, or *Avebury* as it is sometimes spelt, is alluded to by Dr. Stukeley. He tells us it was erected at the time of the death of Sarah; but he is not very clear upon the point, and we leave the statement as it is.

JACOB AND ESAU.

Isaac had two sons, Jacob and Esau. Isaac seems to have had but the one wife, Rebekah of Ur. Josephus describes Isaac as a man beloved of God, living virtuously; and he says "Isaac's sons became a great nation." Rebekah evidently loved Jacob better than Esau. His marriage with the daughters of Heth had grieved her much; and she persuades Isaac to send Jacob to Haran, to the house of Laban her brother; and Isaac called Jacob and blessed him, and charged him, and said unto him: "Thou shalt not take a wife of the daughters of Canaan." And Isaac sent away Jacob, and he went to Padan-Aram, to Laban, son of Bethuel the Syrian, the brother of Rebekah, Jacob and Esau's mother.

We do not read of an angel being sent with Jacob, but we read of the angels of God appearing to him on his way to Haran, or Charron, the burying-place of Terah, which was upon his road; and here he built the first Bethel. "Then Jacob went on his journey, and came into the land of the people of the East"— *not the eastern land, but the land of his people, the people of the East.* "And he looked, and behold a well in the field, and lo, there were three flocks of sheep lying by it, for out of that well they watered the flocks, and a great stone was upon the well's mouth." In a field (*Accad*) by a well (*tub*) he found some men whose language he spoke, for he says, "My brethren, whence be ye? And they said, Of Haran are we." And Jacob knew then that he had reached the home of his mother, the Haran of the "old land." He inquires for Laban, the son of Nahor; "And they said, We know him. And he

said unto them, Is he well? And they said, He is
well : and behold, Rachel his daughter cometh with
the sheep."

A verse in the Book of Ballymote runs thus—

> Beon, Assan, Cassan, three,
> And Ritchel their sister.

Who were these three ancient sons of Ireland, Beon,
Assan, and Cassan, and their sister Ritchel? Surely
they were sons of Laban, the rich shepherd king,
the hard master, whom Jacob served for twenty-one
years. Laban is identified with Bela, of Dinhabah,
King of Edom. In Gen. xxxvi. 31, etc.; and in I.
Chron. i. 43, we find this genealogy:—

"And these are the kings that reigned in the
land of Edom, before there reigned any king over
the children of Israel. And Bela the son of Beor
reigned in Edom, and the name of his city was
Dinhabah. And Bela died, and Jobab the son of
Zerah of Bozrah reigned in his stead. And Jobab
died, and Husham of the land of *Temani* reigned in
his stead. And Husham died, and Hadad the son of
Bedad, who smote *Midian* in the field of Moab,
reigned in his stead; and the name of his city was
Avith. And Hadad died, and Samlah of Masrekah

reigned in his stead. And Samlah died, and Saul of
Rehoboth by the river reigned in his stead. And Saul
died, and Baal-hanan the son of Achbor reigned in
his stead. And Baal-hanan, the son of Achbor, died,
and Hadar reigned in his stead; and the name of his
city was Pau; and his wife's name was Mehetabel,
the daughter of Matred, the daughter of Mezahab."
The names in this genealogy are referable as having
existed in Celtic countries.

There are ten kings in this genealogy, and Dr.
Adam Clarke, in his commentary on them, quotes a
Targum, which refers to the King Bela :—" Balaam,
the impious son of Beor, the same as Laban, the
Syrian, who formed a conspiracy with the sons of
Esau to destroy Jacob and his children ; and he
strived to destroy them utterly. Afterwards, he
reigned in Edom, and the name of his royal city was
Dinhabah, because it was undeservedly given to him."
This Bela, the same Targum says, was killed by
" *Phineas* (we wonder if this was the Phineas Farsaidh
of Irish tradition, the great schoolmaster of the Plains
of Shinar, whose existence is referred to about this
time?) in the wilderness."

The name Edom, in Hebrew, beside meaning a

country, signifies *red*, and is applied to *red* earth. It
also means *Man*, and *Adam*—perhaps in allusion to
him being made out of *Edom* (אדום, and אדם) or
red earth. If there is any difference in the meaning
of the word in Hebrew, it is to be accounted for not
by the simple elision of the letter ו (vaù) in the first
spelling, but by the idiom of the Hebrew language,
that accommodates itself to explain as the same word
sometimes contrary significations of it. Mark, for
instance, the two words אדם, *Adam*, and אדום,
Edom. It is difficult to resist believing that they
meant, if they do not mean, just the same—*Adam*,
or *red earth;* and then were applied more especially
to a country characterised by red earth, or coloured
by the red oxide of iron. The word Edom or Adam
is the story of man made out of *dust.* Now, as the
name may have been thus applied to a country
in the East, presenting to the eye the appearance of
red earth; so it may have been applied to a part of,
or to the British Islands, which, above most countries,
are distinguished by this peculiarity of the soil.

Moab, in the same genealogy, means literally *from
the father.* מ, *from*, אב, *father*, and is another
example of different meanings of the same word, for it

is applied in Gen. xix. 37 to the son of Lot, and in the genealogy as above, signifies the *field of the father.*

If the Targum, as quoted by Dr. Adam Clarke, and again by us from him, be accepted in evidence of Laban being Bela, it throws a great deal of light upon, and assists us to identify the land of Laban. We find the name of Bela or Bala given to a lake, a mountain, and a city in Wales, not far from *Dyne-vor* (in Genesis, *Dinhabah*), another of the names contained in this genealogy. Dynevor has been mentioned by us before, in connection with the tribute of honey to Lud.

The land of the Temanites is also referred to. Dr. Smith says of it :—

"In common with most Edomite names, Teman seems, to have been lost. The occupation of the country by the Nabathaeans seems to have obliterated almost all the traces (always obscure) of the migratory tribes of the desert. True, Eusebius and Jerome mention Teman as a town in their day, distant fifteen miles (according to Eusebius) from Petra, and a Roman post. The identification of the existing *maan* (see Burckhardt) with this Teman may be geographically correct, but it cannot rest upon etymological grounds." As usual, a difficulty besets the commentators, who *must* go to the East for the Scripture sites. If there is no such name as Teman to be found applied to a country or place in the East, surely we cannot err in finding the name and place in Ireland—Teman, or Temora, known by those names from the most remote antiquity—so remote, indeed, that the identification of Teman has been entirely unsuspected by the elaborate writers on Bible history.

Another word in this genealogy is *Midian*, which we have before shown to be one of the old names for Meath. In the twenty-fifth chapter of Genesis we find the names of the children of Abraham by his second wife, Keturah. Among these names is *Midian*, probably the founder of the Midianites of the East. It should be understood that, generally, when we find a name in the west of Europe, with resemblance in spelling, sound, and meaning, to another name in the East, the latter is, according to our view, derived of the former.

Speaking of the Midianites, Dr. Adam Clarke says—"Probably they were those who peopled that part of Arabia-Petrea contiguous to the land of

Moab, eastward of the *Dead Sea.*" It is astonishing to find so much that is *"probable"* in the writings of even the most acute Bible scholars. Not that we doubt the locality of *these* Midianites.

Josephus says—"The city, Midian, which lay upon the *Red Sea*—;" from which we take it that there is considerable uncertainty as to where it was.

In the neighbourhood of Meath there is a parish named *Saul,* also one of the names in the genealogy quoted. Saul was a King of Edom, and Baal-hanan, another name mentioned in it, was his successor. As to Baal-hanan there are numerous names of places in Ireland that contain the most of this word. We will not point to any extra significance in the word Bally-shannon; nor say that the "City of *Pau,*" because it is not to be found in the East, is therefore by the Pyrenees—but why is it not found in the East?

We have something more to say of Jacob, and now return to him. He is sent by his father Isaac "to Padan-Aram unto Laban, son of Bethuel the Syrian" (Gen. xxviii. 5.)

Syria simply means *Aram.* Padan-Aram, in the Welsh translation of the Bible, is substituted for the word *Mesopotamia,* as meaning almost the same thing—*country between rivers.* But it is remarkable that there is a *Padan's Causeway* on the coast of Wales, not far from Dinebah; also a village in the neighbourhood, called *St. Padan's*, and a mountain bearing the same name. In Ireland there is St. Padan's Well, in connection with which there are many marvels recorded. We give these names but it is for the ingenious to decide as to whether there were a people of Padan-Aram in Western Europe in the habit of giving names to the places in which they dwelt, or to the places merely visited, or as it might be, won by them.

The Padan-Aram to which Jacob came was well stocked with "Flocks and herds, speckled and spotted cattle, sheep and goats." On this we have to say that there is no more remarkable fact to our mind than that the British Islands, above any quarter in the world, are celebrated for their *spotted* and *speckled* cattle. There is another fact: the country in which Jacob sojourned for twenty years was one in which grew chestnut, hazel, and green-poplar; these are not Eastern trees, but native of these islands. Commentators tell us hazel must mean the *almond-tree*, and chestnut the *plane-tree*, but of course these explanations do not alter the text of Genesis xxx. 37 : "And Jacob took him rods of green poplar, and of the hazel and chestnut-tree, and pilled white strakes in them, and made the white appear which was in the rods." The Celtic bards speak of the "rods of the prophets of the secluded dales," and it is a fact that the Druid-priests were in the habit of using *hazel* rods for divining purposes.* The peeling of rods for recording events was a common practice of the Druids, perhaps instituted by Jacob, perhaps learnt by him of them.

The wood tables of the bards—what were they? Peeled and unpeeled rods, fastened together in a frame, on which, as a table, the records of those days were kept. The *rod of office*, the rod of the Magician, the rod of Moses, Aaron's rod, the *lituus* of the Roman Augur, the Freemason's rod, and many other rods of authority are to be traced back to these early times.

The "Holy White House" on the Taff, at Caedydd (Cardiff), as well as the first church of Glastonbury, was built of peeled white rods.

Mr. Rawlinson, talking of the mineral resources of

* The miners of Wales and Cornwall use in the present day hazel rods *for the discovery* of minerals.

the supposed neighbourhood of Ur, says : "The alluvium is wholly destitute of metals, and even of stone." He also tells us : "No permanent streams water this region ; occasional wadys or torrent courses, only full after heavy rains, are found; but the scattered inhabitants depend for water chiefly on their wells, which are deep and numerous, but yield only a scanty supply of a brackish and unpalatable fluid. No settled population can at any time have found sustenance in this region, which only produces a few dates, and in places a poor, unsucculent herbage. Sandstorms are frequent, and at other times the fearful simoon sweeps across the entire tract, destroying with its breath both men and animals.

But if man by long residence becomes thoroughly inured to these regions, it is otherwise with the animal creation. Camels sicken, and birds are so distressed by the high temperature, that they sit in the date-trees in Bagdad, with their mouths open, panting for fresh air."

Although we pity the birds in the date-trees of Bagdad under high temperature, and believe Mr. Rawlinson *enlivens* by their sufferings his otherwise anything but pleasant picture.

If we must understand Mr. Rawlinson as describing the neighbourhood of Ur, or Chaldæa, wholly destitute of metals and even of stones, how was it possible that Jacob could erect the "heap of witnesses," or stones, *Jegar-sahadutha:* called by him *Galeed.*

"And Jacob took a stone, and set it up for a pillar. And Jacob said unto his brethren, Gather stones; and they took stones, and made an heap, and they did eat there upon the heap." (Gen. xxxi. 45, 46.)

We think there is almost sufficient in our remarks upon these quotations to show that it was in the highest degree improbable that there was scarcity of stones in Ur or Chaldæa.

But let us see how the first peculiarity of the place, as described, agrees with the Ur and Chaldæa of the Bible. We are informed that the neighbourhood of Ur and Chaldæa was entirely destitute of metals. Then, from what sources were the metals taken of which the people of this quarter manufactured their weapons of war—their swords and shields, &c. ? No metals there ! then there never was prosperity there. But we know that it was the region of two of the greatest monarchies that ever existed—Babylcn and Nineveh. Had it not even bronze or iron ? We

are sensible that it is impossible to point to a nation
that ever became great without using one or the
other, or both, of these metals. Sir Robert Kane, in
his excellent work, "The Industrial Resources of
Ireland,"* says upon this point :—

"A nation without iron cannot emerge from a
state of semi-barbarism. Its chiefs may be magnificent in gold and jewels, its warriors may be armed
with shields and swords of bronze, on which the labour
of long-practised workmen bestow a finish, admirable
even at the present day, but the rarity and cost, as
well of material as of artificers, deprives the general
population of all power to render those precious
metals available to their domestic comfort. It is only
when iron is obtainable, when cheap and abundant, it
places within the reach of all the means of constructing
the various tools and instruments, by which the arts
and agriculture are so materially advanced, that civilization can become so firmly grounded amongst a
people. . . . . .

"Some centuries ago Ireland presented a picture of
manufacturing industry . . . . . Covered with
forests, and possessing iron ore of the highest purity

* Cap. III.

in great abundance, Ireland was sprinkled over with small iron works, in which the wood charcoal was employed, and thus iron manufactured of excellent quality; in fact, such as we now import from Sweden and Russia for all the finer purposes of cutlery and mechanism. Such kind of iron furnaces may be considered as now belonging but to the history of art."

As the basis of prosperity is the proper working and use of metals, so we must conclude, in accordance with the tenor of our argument, that the British Islands, and particularly Ireland, were the seats of the earliest civilizations that spread eastward to the Tigris and Euphrates.

The neighbourhood of Ur, according to Rawlinson and those who precede him, we must take to have been Chaldæa, and the country east of the Tigris and west of the Euphrates, embracing the extent of modern Bagdad. The Pashalic of Bagdad stretches north-west from the head of the Persian Gulf, lat. about 30° to 38° N., long. 40° and 48° E. ; on the south-west bounded by the Arabian desert, east by Persia, and north by the Pashalics of Vau and Diarbekir. It is thus about 630 miles long, and about 450 at its greatest breadth, traversed by the Euphrates

and Tigris, which afterwards unite, and enter the
Persian Gulf in one stream. It is generally divided
thus : The land lying between the Tigris and Euphrates '(the supposed ancient Chaldæa, or Mesopotamia, or Aram Naharam, &c.), that east of the Tigris,
and that west of the Euphrates. The first is now a
complete desert, the second is fertile, and the third
flat and sandy. The usual explanations of the barren
state of the land between the rivers is, that it is caused
by the wretched government of the Turks.

Mr. Rawlinson says about Bagdad that " *No settled
population can have found sustenance at any time in this
region.*" The italics are ours. Now, is it possible he
can be serious, and so far forget, for the sake of
saying this, that (according to himself, beside every
other writer upon the subject) a settled population *did*
exist there, and there for many centuries must have
found sustenance. It is quite true that all the
necessaries and luxuries of the rival empires of
Babylon and Nineveh may not have 'been produced
within the area of the country as we give it—just as
the necessaries and luxuries of modern civilizations do
not depend upon their own internal resources. Even
in an era anterior, as some say, to the building success

M

of these ancient kingdoms, we find mention made of a place to the east of them celebrated for its trade ramifications; we mean Bactria. Babylon and Nineveh while trading a good deal yet depended upon their own resources for supplies of the necessaries of life.

We cannot believe for a moment that man in his first and natural state forces himself to settle in barren and unpromising situations. He is more likely to select for his habitat a place that has at least the smile of nature upon it; but what an uncomfortable feeling one experiences endeavouring to *fancy* what Mr. Rawlinson pictures of the country and district of the immortal Ninevite and Babylonian monarchies! Nothing from their own and adjacent country to eat but a few dates, and in places only a poor unsucculent herbage, we suppose not sufficient for their cattle to exist upon. It cannot have been so.

But the miseries of hunger were not relieved by even a fair supply of clean water; for it is manifest from our author that " No permanent streams watered the country, that the wells there yielded only a scanty supply of brackish and unpalatable fluid."

Surely his description of the resources and climate

of the old Chaldæa and its neighbourhood does prove either that it and the surrounding places are wrongly described, or that Mr. Rawlinson is telling us of some other part of the earth, in which it was impossible for the human family to multiply, let alone prosper.

But we must believe that there was a Babylon and a Nineveh in the East, just as we believe and have endeavoured to show, the probability of their being settled in by a people from the Shinar of Genesis, the old land that contained the Chaldæa, the Ur of the Chaldees, and other important places, that have been known by name only to scholars, but which were not dreamt of as having reference to Europe.

The district of Ur and Chaldæa must have been of a salubrious climate, fertile, and with mineral resources of its own, or it is impossible that civil and material greatness could have developed there. And when we reflect upon the speech of the people of Chaldæa, the Hebrew speech, and their monuments, and find their similarities, and often their identifications in the Celtic tongue and mohuments, we cannot reasonably resist the inference that, as we cast our eye over Europe and the north of Africa into Asia, the first migration of the human family went forth from a fruitful and favoured region in the west of Europe, and not from the almost unearthly land as described by Rawlinson.

We here quote from an old author what he says about the brooks and springs of a more genial district, a district that has furnished throughout these pages some remarkable evidences of its identity as Ur of the Chaldees.

Gerard Bote, writing as far back as 1650,* says :— "Ireland is very full of them everywhere, not only in the mountainous and hilly parts, but even in the flat and Champain countries, which springs for the most part are all of one and the same fashion, being like unto a small pitfull of water up to the brim, at the lower side whereof the water doth run forth, without making any noise or bubbling. . . . . . The water of these well-springs is for the most part cool, clear, and pure, *free from all strange smell and taste—(not brackish* and unpalatable fluid this!)" And again, "No country in the world is fuller of brooks

---

* " Ireland's Natural History," p. 54.

than Ireland, where the same be numberless, and water all parts of the land on all sides."

As we have said before, Ireland is perhaps above any place to be distinguished as the country of *wells*, —the land of *tob*, or of wells, referred to in the Koran, and in the xi. 3 of Judges, and elsewhere. *Galeed-*Mizpah (Gen. xxxi. 48, 49) was on a mountain in Ur of the Chaldees, and is to be distinguished from the Gileads (for there were two) of Canaan. The Gilead of Ur was a place of solemn covenant and witness between Laban and Jacob. The land of *Tob* then was a portion of the Ancient Chaldæa, situated in the east—of the Atlantic !—it was the country now known as Ireland.

The Gilead spoken of in Judges was a Gilead of Canaan, which we leave where it is placed in the east of the Mediterranean.

Jacob, before he had reached the land of his birth, was reproached by his uncle Laban (who made up to him at Mount Gilead, after seven days' pursuit) for stealing away secretly from his house with all his (Jacob's) wives, children, cattle, and camels. Laban speaks to him :—

" Why did'st thou not tell me, that I might have

sent thee away with mirth and with songs, with tabret and with *harp?*"

The word *harp* occurring in this passage indicates that it was in use at this very remote period with Laban in Ur. Of course some will say that the harp is to be found on many of the Egyptian, and some of the Persian and Median monuments, and that, therefore, Laban must have used the expression from a custom that was introduced among his people from one or other of those countries. But the progress of Ethnology is not yet sufficiently advanced to decide that Asia was the source of European population. Until it does settle this question—a conclusion, by the way, not likely to be ever arrived at—we must hold that the people of Asia had their first customs and institutions, their religion, speech, and first impressions from the western quarter of Shinar, or Europe.

The reference to the camels here bears upon what we have said elsewhere about the figures of them to be found upon the monuments of Ireland and Scotland. ·

Among those that went with Jacob were eleven of his children, most of whose names remain in the

British Islands, principally in the names of places. His first wife Leah, rendered by Josephus *Lea*, is a common name in England of rivers, villages, and towns, as well as of people. Reu, or Reuben, is as common both as a christian and surname. Simeon, one of his sons, leaves his name, in many cases unaltered, in forms also that proves at once their origin; thus, Simmons, Simmonds, Simeon, Symon, Simonite, etc. Levi, another son of his, may be remembered by our reader as having been referred to with Lewis, Levison, and other families.* Judah, also a son of Reuben, is found in the forms Jude, Judd, Judson, etc. Issachar was another son. There was a place in Yorkshire called *Ischa*, and another in Wales. Dan is the next son, and there are many examples of the name to be found everywhere in Western Europe. Danmonia was the ancient name of Devonshire and a part of Cornwall. Denmark is supposed to have been called after the people of Danæ, a Scythian tribe who settled there, whom some have alleged to be the same as the Tuath-de-Danan, a colony that went to Ireland before the Milesians, and who were people of Dan. The Dedan

* Page 127.

of Ezek. xxv. 13, xxvii. 20, from its proximity to Teman, must have been in Ireland. Of Gad, another son, we have before referred to. Ashir comes next, and we find his name preserved in that of a place in the north of Scotland—the Devynock of *Ashir.* Zebulon, the last name of the sons of Jacob we quote here, is to be found in the name of a place on the coast of Cornwall, called *St. Perin Zabuloe,* which became an oratory or house of prayer near the sea. It was covered over by the sands, and lost to sight for hundreds of years, but is now restored, and is an object of great interest.

We have noticed that *Gilead*-Mizpah was on a mountain in Ur of the Chaldees, and by that we mean that this Gilead was in Ireland.* Now we find that Jacob, on this mount of Gilead, took a stone and set it up for a pillar. It is not a little remarkable that

---

* As to the uncertainty of the location of Gilead, we give the following from Calmet :—"Gilead is often put for the whole country beyond Jordan." From Smith's Dict. of the Bible we take—"There is no evidence in fact that any particular mountain was meant by Mount Gilead . . . . the first notice we have of the name Gilead is in connection with the history of Jacob (Gen. xxxi. 21, sq.) ; but it is probably the same which is referred to under the name *Ham,* and was inhabited by the giant Zuzims" (Gen. xiv. 5).

on the mound of Tara was a stone, so sacred and valuable, that it was the custom for many centuries to crown the kings of Ireland sitting upon it. This stone was called the *Lia Fail*, or *Stone of Destiny*. Beside this, it has had the name of *Jacob's Stone* from time immemorial. Some Jewish scholars are of opinion that it is the identical stone on which the patriarch dreamed of Luz (Gen. xxviii. 19).

"And Jacob rose up early in the morning, and took the stone that he had put for his pillow, and set it up for a pillar " (Gen. xxviii. 18).

LEGEND OF THE LIA FAIL; OR, STONE OF

DESTINY.

As Ireland was called Inis-Fail, or the Island of Destiny, by the Tuath-de-Danans, so had the stone they are said to have brought with them been called *Lia Fail*, or the Stone of Destiny. The ancient Kings of Ireland, both of the Danan and Milesian race, used to sit upon it when being crowned.

This stone was sent to Scotland in the sixth century for the coronation of Fergus, who was of the Milesian race, and was used for many centuries at the coronation of the Scottish Kings at Scone; from the abbey of which place it was taken by Edward I. in his wars with Scotland, and conveyed to Westminster Abbey, where it has since remained. It is called Jacob's Stone from him, as it is said, having rested his head upon it during his sleep at Bethel, or Luz. Bethel, or Luz, was in Canaan; and there Jacob planted a *pillar* before his departure for Ur, which shows that a *second* pillar he left behind him in Ireland; for the first was in Luz, before his coming to the country of his forefathers; the second was in Ur before he left it to plant a third on his return to Canaan (Gen. xxxv. 14).

Dr. O'Connor, in his account of the Irish MSS. at Stowe, states that the Lia Fail was at a remote period removed from the royal Rath or mound at Tara, and taken to the kings at Cruachan, in Connaught, and that because of that it ceased to emit its usual sound called *Ges*, which signifies a spell or charm. It was supposed to have been profaned by Cuchulain, who resented its silence when, according to a note in the "Annals of the Four Masters," his friend, Fiacha Fionn, was appointed monarch of Ireland, in the beginning of the first century, and the stone did not resume its accustomed sound until the inauguration of Con of the Hundred Battles, in the second century, he being a legitimate monarch.

In the beginning of the sixth century Murtogh Mac Earca, who was then reigning monarch of Ireland, had a brother named Fergus Mac Earca, who became king of the Irish colonies, and settled in Dalriada in Albany, afterwards called Scotland. He requested his brother to send over the Lia Fail that he might be crowned upon it, and so feel, in accordance with belief in the power of the stone, secure upon his throne.

Some say, with O'Flaherty in his Ogygia, that the Stone of Destiny was not taken to Scotland until the ninth century, when Aodh Finliath, King of Ireland, sent it to Kenneth Mac Alpin, his father-in-law, who was crowned King of Scotland.

Keating and Charles O'Connor mention the Lia Fail. The former gives a version in Irish of the old rhyme attaching to it :—

> Cineadh Scuit, saor an fhine
> Munbudh breag an fhaisdine
> Mar a fuighid an Lia Fail
> Dlighid flaithea do ghabhail.

This is the English of it :

> Unless the fixed decrees of Fate give way,
> The Scots shall govern and the sceptre sway,
> Where e'er this stone they find and its dread sound obey.

Hector Bœtius renders it into Latin :

> Ne fallat fatum, Scoti, quocunque locatum
> Invenient lapidem hunc, regnare tenentur ibidem.

Thus translated :

> If fate's decrees be not announced in vain,
> Where e'er this stone is found the Scots shall reign.

This stone was preserved with the greatest care and veneration in Scotland, from the sixth to the thirteenth century, and was looked upon by her people as the palladium of their kingdom, from a very ancient prophecy, that the Scotch or Milesian race would continue to rule while it was in their possession. It was kept first at the Monastery of St. Columkille, at Iona, in the Hebrides, afterwards at Dunstaffnage, in Argyleshire, the earliest royal seat of Scottish kings of the Irish race. Perhaps the reason that O'Flaherty believes it was not taken from Ireland until the ninth century, was his mistaking its removal from the Monastery of St. Columkille, at Iona, to Scone, by Kenneth MacAlpin, king of Scotland, and conqueror of the Picts.

Connellan observes that "some have considered that it was first brought to Ireland by the Danaus from the Cave of Canaan." Hence the name of Jacob's stone. We need not reiterate our opinion here that it was one of *three* stones set up by Jacob.

It is strange how opinions vary about this stone. Some writers, notably Dr. Petrie, have told us that the stone has never been removed from Ireland, and that it is actually yet to be seen standing upright on one of the mounds of Tara. But the majority and the most trustworthy of Irish and Scotch antiquaries have proved it to be no other than that let into the coronation chair at Westminster Abbey.

" It is one primeval monument which binds together the whole Empire. The iron rings, the battered surface, the crack which has all but rent its solid mass asunder, bear witness to its long migrations. It is thus embedded in the heart of the English monarchy—an element of poetic, patriarchal, heathen times, which, like Araunah's rocky threshing-floor in the midst of the Temple of Solomon, carries back our thoughts to races and customs now almost extinct; a link which unites the throne of England to the traditions of Tara and Iona, and connects the chain of our complex civilisation with the forces of our mother earth, the stocks and stones of savage nature."[*] Dean Stanley makes Will Rishanger the oldest writer upon the subject of the Lia Fail—he confines himself to Scottish accounts only, and, of course, loses the advantage of the older Irish references to it. It is strange how the reverend and learned gentleman has been led like most of the writers of Scottish history to refer to the statement of Rishanger, that "Milo, king of the Scots in Spain, gave it to his favourite son, *Simon Brek,* the first king of the Scots in Ireland, and that Simon Brek placed it in Tara, where it remained until it was brought by Fergus, the son of Erch or Ferchard."

All Irish accounts agree that *Milo,* as Milesius is here termed, had only three sons, Heber, Heremon, and Jar. No one knows at the present time from what fertile brain was born Simon Brek. Was there ever in the flesh a king of the Celts, or of any nation of them, named Simon Brek? The name simply means the speckled sun, or firmament, from *Samen,* the sun, and *Brach,* speckled.

---

[*] Stanley's " Memorials of Westminster Abbey," pp. 67, 68.

Philo Byblius mentions a Baal-Samen, to which the Syrians and Canaanites lifted up their hands.

Saman, in Irish mythology, signifies the Divinity, who presided at the judgment of departed souls.

When writers of Scottish history, and interpreters of her tradition, agree to divest themselves of national prejudice, they will, and not till then, look to Ireland for an explanation of matters that chiefly illustrate the early history of the Scot.

Fergus, who succeeded in getting the Lia Fail over to Scotland, is quoted by Dean Stanley, and others beside, as son of *Erch*, or Earc, as it is given in Irish; but this Erch, or Earc, has no older meanings than "The Sun," "Heaven," "Speckled," &c., and may be—indeed, we believe it is—only another spelling of the word *Brach*. For various meanings of the word, see O'Rielly's Dictionary. The phrase *Simon Brek* was misunderstood as meaning a king. It may, however, have been applied as a cognomen to some early king; thus it would be a very natural way of expressing admiration of a good and wise monarch to say that he was the *light* or the *sun* of the *firmament*, or of *heaven*—he was Simon Brek!

In some respects what is narrated of the pillow of

Jacob, strangely coincides with what we are told of St. Columba's pillow. Jacob slept upon his stone pillow and had a dream, in which he saw the angels of God, ascending and descending, from heaven to earth and from earth to heaven. Visions of angels and of heaven seem also to have formed the primary notion in connection with St. Columba's pillow of stone, preserved for a long time as a monument beside his grave.

Cumine, the White, the successor of St. Columba (or St. Columkille, according to the usual spelling), in the Monastery of Iona, and Adamnan, the Abbot of the same place, from A.D. 679 to 704, speak of the stone at Iona, or St. Columba's pillow. Adamnan follows Cumine in nearly the same words, and tells us how visions of angels floated before St. Columba's eyes in death; how his church was lighted up by their glory, and that, as they carried his soul to heaven, they illumined with their splendour the sky over the sea, and unto Donegal and Tyrone.

The two accounts may refer to different stone pillows; at any rate, the best authorities have traced, to almost a certainty, the stone of Tara, Iona (it was deposited in Iona when it first was received from

Ireland), and Scone, to Westminster Abbey, to which place it has been ever since the time of Edward I.

That the people of London prized the stone much we have ample evidence, for when the Scots showed they cherished the hope of recovering it, the Londoners gave it unmistakeable attachment, no doubt influenced by the mystery and sacredness believed to have belonged to it from the time of Jacob. Dean Stanley gives an account of this :—

" A solemn article in the Treaty of Northampton, which closed the long war between the two countries, required the restoration of the lost relics to Scotland. Accordingly Edward III., then residing at Bardesley, directed his writ under the privy seal to the Abbot and Convent of Westminster, commanding them to give the stone for this purpose to the Sheriffs of London, who would receive the same from them by indenture,* and cause it to be carried to the Queen-mother. All the other articles of the treaty were fulfilled. Even the " Black Rood," the sacred cross of Holyrood, which Edward I. had carried off with the other relics, was restored. But the stone of Scone, on which the kings of Scotland used at Scone to be

---

* *Statuta Ecclesiæ Scotiam*, pref. p. xlvi.

N

placed on their inauguration, the people of London would by no means whatever allow to depart from · themselves."*

GEOLOGICAL ACCOUNT OF THE CORONATION STONE.

BY PROFESSOR A. C. RAMSAY, LL.D., F.R.S.,

Director of the Geological Survey of England, &c., &c., June 19, 1865

AT the request of the Dean of Westminster, I joined a party for the purpose of examining the Coronation Stone in Westminster Abbey, in June, 1865. The following remarks are the results of my observations :—

The Coronation Stone consists of a dull reddish or purplish sandstone, with a few small embedded pebbles. One of these is of quartz, and two others of a dark material, the nature of which I was unable to ascertain. They may be Lydian stone. The rock is calcareous, and is of the kind that masons would call "freestone." Chisel marks are visible on one or more of its sides. A little mortar was in the sockets in which the iron rings lie, apparently not of very ancient date. To my eye the stone appears as if it had originally been prepared for building purposes, but had never been used.

It is very difficult to settle the geological formation to which any far transported mass of stone may belong, especially when

---

* Chronicle of Lanercost, p. 261 ; Maitland, p. 146.

the history of the mass is somewhat vague in its earlier stages. The country around Scone is formed of old red sandstone, and the tints of different portions of that formation are so various, that it is quite possible the Coronation Stone may have been derived from one of its strata. The country round Dunstaffnage also consists of old red sandstone, reddish or purplish in hue, and much of it is conglomerate near Oban, Dunolly, and in other places. In McCulloch's "Western Isles of Scotland" there is a note (at p. 112, vol. ii.) in which, writing of the Coronation Stone, he says:—"The stone in question is a calcareous sandstone, exactly resembling that which forms the doorway at Dunstaffnage Castle." There can be little doubt that the castle was built of the rocks of the neighbourhood, the sandstone strata of which are described in a letter now before me, by my colleague, Mr. Geskie, as dull reddish or purplish. This precisely agrees with the character of the Coronation Stone itself. McCulloch does not mention how he ascertained how the stone in question (The Coronation Stone) is calcareous. This description, however, is correct. When the stone was placed on the table in the Abbey the lower part of it was swept with a soft brush, and as many grains of sand were thus detached from the stone as would cover a sixpence.

Among these was a minute fragment of the stone itself. These were tested for me in Dr. Percy's laboratory by Mr. Ward, and found to be slightly calcareous. The red colouring matter is peroxide of iron. There can be no doubt that the stone dust brushed off the lower surface of the stone truly represents the matter of which the mass is composed. It was simply loosened by old age, and when examined with the magnifying glass, showed grains of quartz and a few small scales of mica, precisely similar to those observed in the stone itself.

On the whole, I incline to think (with McCulloch) that the doorway of Dunstaffnage Castle may have been derived from the same parent rock, though as there are plenty of red sandstone in Ireland (from where it is said to have been brought), it may be impossible to prove precisely its origin.

It is extremely improbable that the stone has been derived from any of the rocks of the Hill of Tara, from whence it is said to have been transported to Scotland, for they, on the authority of Mr. Jukes, Director of the Geological Survey of Ireland, are of carboniferous age, and (as explained in one of the memoirs of the Irish survey, do not present the texture of red colour so characteristic of the Coronation Stone.

Neither could it have been taken from the rocks of Iona, which, on the authority of my colleague, Mr. Geikie, consist of a flaggy micaceous grit of gneiss. There is no red sand-stone on it, so far as I know ; indeed, I am quite sure there is none.

That it belonged to the rocks originally around Bethel is equally unlikely, since, according to all creditable reports, they are formed of strata of limestone.

The rocks of Egypt, as far as I know, consist of nummulitic limestone, of which the Great Pyramid is built, and though we know of crystalline rocks (such as syenite, etc.) in Egypt, I have never heard of any strata occurring there similar to the red sandstone of the Coronation Stone.

Dean Stanley expresses himself upon this—" The conclusions . . . . . are as follows :—The stone is certainly from Scotland, probably from Scone."

We have given the above account of the geological examination of what is called the *Stone of Scone*, in order to show that there has been considerable interest manifested in this old relic, even by scientific investi-gators ; but it is not a little strange that we find them concluding so erroneously from their own facts as to the elements of the stone, and their admission that there is "plenty of red sandstone in Ireland." And when we know that the early history of the stone is taken from Irish sources it is rather illogical, not to say reprehensible, on the part of Professor A. C. Ramsey, and those he joined, "for the purpose of examining the Coronation Stone," to lead the good Dean Stanley to conclude that "the stone is certainly from Scotland, probably from Scone"—unless he means that—since it was taken to Westminster.

Jacob, after erecting the Pillar of Witness between himself and Laban, "offered sacrifice upon the mount," and called his brethren to eat bread, which they did while tarrying all night in the mount.

And early in the morning Laban rose up and kissed his sons and daughters, and blessed them, and Laban departed and returned unto his place.—Gen. xxxi., 54, 55. And Jacob went on his way, and the angels of God met him; and when Jacob saw them he said : "This is God's host, and he called the name of that place *Mahanaim.*—xxxii., 1, 2. This place, *Mahanaim*, brings us to consider with it another name we find in Cap. xxxi. 47—we mean *Jegar-Sahadutha.*

Mahanaim,* Gen. xxxii. 2. In *Heb.* מחנים. Jegar-
Sahadutha,† Gen. xxxi. 47.

The above is what is said on these two names by the
learned editors of the new edition of the Bible. The
equivalent of the word *Galeed*, according to these authorities, is *Jegar-Sahadutha*. In this form it is capable of
explanation in Irish thus :—*Gall* (often in Celtic, as

---

* That is, "two hosts," or "camps." Some have believed
the dual is here used for the plural ; others that Jacob thought of
his own camp and the camp of angels. (So Abenezra, and after
him Clericus). More likely the angels were encamped on the
right hand and on the left, so seeming to surround and protect
Jacob (see on V. I.) The place called Mahanaim was in the
tribe of Gad, and was assigned to the Levites.—Jos. xxi. 38.
The name *Mahneh* is still retained in the *supposed* site of the
ancient town (Robinson).

There was of the sect of the Essenians one named *Manahem*,
which seems very like Mahanaim.

† Jegar-Sahadutha is the Aramaic (Chaldee or Syraic) equivalent for the Hebrew Galeed, both meaning the "heap of witness."
It appears, therefore, that at this time Jacob spoke Hebrew,
whilst his uncle Laban spoke Syraic. We can only account for
this by supposing either that the family of Nahor originally
spoke Syraic, and that Abraham and his descendants learned
Hebrew in Canaan, where evidently the Hebrew language was
indigenous when he first went there, having probably been
acquired by the Hanutic Canaanites, from an earlier Semitic
race—or else, which is not otherwise supported, that the ances-
tors of Laban having left the early seat of the family had
unlearned their original Hebrew, and acquired the Syraic dialect
of Padan-Aram."—Notes from new edition of Bible.

before noticed) *stone*, as *lia* from the genetive *liag*, (W. *lech*). The cause of this seems to have originated from the stone altar—the altar of burnt sacrifice—being called *gall* and *liag*, each word expressing both *fire* and *stone*, or *stone altar*. There is a word in Irish that signifies "a heap," it is *leaċd* (leaċt), but it is quite possible to perceive the meaning of Galeed without its aid—ᵹall-leaᵹ, which both expresses *fire* and *stone*, or *stone* and *fire*, or *stone* and *stone*, so have we *Galeed*, or the heap of *stones*, which may be taken in a figurative sense to mean something to *mark* or *witness*—therefore the "heap of witness." This is the more likely as there cannot be found in the Hebrew a more satisfactory explanation of the word. גל, *gal*, in Parkhurst, means, among other things, a "roundish heap of stones, or the like rolled or tumbled together." That we have offered a better and truer explanation of the word Galeed—said to have its equivalent in the Aramaic (Chaldee or Syraic) word, *Jegar-Sahadutha*—we will leave to the sense of the reader.

We now direct our attention more particularly to Esau.

The people of Israel kept an account of their father Jacob, but of Esau, save the names of the dukes who were his sons and grandsons, there is little or no information in the Mosaic account.

After the death of Isaac, Jacob is found in possession of the land of Canaan.

" And Esau took his wives and his sons, and his daughters, and all the persons of his house, and all his substance which he had got in the land of Canaan, and went into the country from the face of his brother Jacob.

" For their riches were more than that they might dwell together; and the land wherein they were strangers could not bear them because of their cattle.

" Thus dwelt Esau in Mount Seir, Esau is Edom." Gen. xxxvi. 6, 7, 8.

The parting of Laban and Jacob took place in 1739 B.C.; the migration of Esau in 1740 B.C., in which year he takes possession of a Mount Seir, clearly not the Seir he had resided in, for that was in Canaan.

The above verses are followed by a list of the generations of Esau, and the geneology of the Edomite kings before referred to, who possessed Temen, Midian, and Dinebah; the king of the latter mentioned place, the Targum, as we have shown, identifies with Laban. Laban made a solemn covenant on Mount Gilead with Jacob, and he is said by the Targum to have broken it, and formed a compact with Esau to destroy the children of Jacob. Let us conjecture how this may have happened. Jacob left Laban, taking with him great riches—flocks and herds, sheep and goats, and camels, and money; and although Esau had accepted his present, yet we are not justified in believing that he had altogether forgotten that his brother had taken away his blessing and his birthright.

Laban and Esau had each a grievance, and it did not require much to make them break the covenant they had separately made with Jacob, so they may have compacted to destroy his children.

We do not read anywhere of the death or burial place of Esau; but we gather from the prophets, Amos, Jeremiah, Obadiah, Ezekiel, and Isaiah, that the sin of Edom was breaking the brotherly covenant, and that the punishment was with "Fire upon Teman." " The cry, the noise thereof is heard in the Red Sea." Jer. xx. 21. The punishment of Edom was evidently by *earthquake*—the earthquake prophesied by Amos, and referred to by the other prophets retrospectively.

Calmet says—"It is a tradition in the East, that
in the time of Abdon,* judge of the Hebrews, a colony
of Edomites settled in Italy, that Latinus reigned
amongst them; that Romulus derived his origin from
them. The most famous Rabbins obstinately mention this tradition. The Talmud calls Italy and Rome
"The most cruel empire of Edom." The Jews assert
that the Edomites having embraced Christianity under
Constantine, got to Rome and "into the Roman
empire; others say that an Idumean priest brought
Christianity into Rome."

The Edomites are associated with Sier and Mount
Sier. The Sier in Canaan would seem to have
received its name from Sier in ancient Chaldæa. At
any rate we find the Horites, a people spoken of in
connection with Mount Sier, anterior to the time of
Jacob and Esau.

There is a word used by some writers as synony-
mous with Sier, it is Gebal. Calmet says that—
"Gebal, instead of Mount Sier, sometimes put Mount
Gebla. Eusebius and Jerome frequently mention

---

* We find St. Abdon classed amongst the Saints of the
Roman calendar; also some Mosaic-Scripture names — St.
Abraham, St. Job, St. Aaron, St. Daniel, St. Asaph, St.
David, St. Gummar or Gomar, &c.

the Gebaline in Idumea, and its capital Petra. Gebal signifies a mountain, and the denomination not ancient, since it appears only in Psalm lxxxiii. 7, which in our opinion was only written in the time of Josephat, king of Judah."

Smith, speaking on the same subject, says—" The contexts of this Psalm and of the historical records, will justify our assuming the Gebal of the Psalms to be one and the same city with the Gebal of Ezekiel, and not another, as some have supposed, in the dis- trict, which is by Josephus, Eusebius, and St. Jerome called Gebaline. The Gibal of Ezekiel was no mean city, from the fact that its inhabitants are written *Giblites*, and *Biblians*, in the Vulgate; and in the LXX., we may infer their identity with the Gebalites spoken of in connection with Lebanan. Josh. xiii. 5; Ezek. viii. 13; Kings ii. 5, 18; Ezek. xxvii. 9."

In the Irish and Erse dictionaries the word *Sier*, as we find it in the Bible, is given in the first as *Sier, west, occidental;* and in the latter as *Siar, west, west- ward;* therefore it is most likely to have been used in this sense by the Hebrews, who would indicate by it the western portion of their country in Europe. Unless this was actually the case, how shall we account for the word having this signification in the Irish? Was it the Hebrew contributed this word to the Irish vocabulary, or contrariwise, the Irish to the Hebrew vocabulary?—in one or other of these ways the word must have come into use. As to the place called Siar, Hebrew lexicons merely tell us that it is the name of a place in the East, some of them putting it in Canaan, and others merely referring to it as a place mentioned in the Bible.

The other word, *Gabhal*, understood to have the same signification as *Sier*, is noticed by Vallency and others as the primitive form of the word *Gael*. If it be so, we can see little difficulty in understanding that *Gaedhal* (pronounced *Gael*) may have in process of time softened into *Gabhal*, and was then pronounced with the *b* silent, admitting of the same pronunciation as *Gael*. No one will dispute that the Gaels have, from the most remote antiquity, been in the main inhabiting the west of Europe; these words, then, being synonymous, it may be assumed that Sier was another of those places that existed in the west of Europe, but which, through some undefined cause, and in the confusion of history, has remained unknown to Bible scholars, who, as we have shewn, almost invariably search the East only for the places mentioned in Scripture.

Most of the descendants of Esau and his long line of Dukes, settled in South Western Europe, but some of them returned to Canaan. From Exodus xv. 15, we find that Moses makes mention of the Dukes of Edom,* which shews that they were in existence in his time. In Num. xx. 21, we read of a King of Edom, not a Duke, refusing to give Israel passage through his border. The title of Duke, like most other titles of honour, often at first signified some one distinguished for his mental qualities, after which his immediate descendant inherited the title, who may not have been distinguished by any remarkable excellence of mind. So the word אַלּוּף Aleph,† translated into English *Duke*, meant originally *"leader*," a *chief*, a man recognised by his tribe as their head in mental as well as physical quality. The Irish *Ollam* may be understood in the same sense, and sometimes applied to a doctor of law, as in the Gaelic *Oileamh* or *Ollamh*.

---

* " The Dukes of Edom shall be amazed."

† The *Caliph* of the Arabians remains, another form of the word, meaning the same thing.

These dukes are descendants of Sier, as well as of Esau, whom "the Mahometans call *Ais* (Bib. Orient., p. 80), and add some particulars to his history, as that Jacob, having by surprise obtained the blessing from Isaac, Esau desired his father to beg of God to produce kings and conquerors from his family, since he had prayed for Jacob that saints and prophets should issue from him. This Isaac would not refuse, and God gave Esau a son named *Roum*, from whom descended the Greek and Roman emperors " *(Calmet)*. In Ezekiel xxvii. 9, there is mention made of the "ancients of Gebal; and the *wise men* thereof were in thee, thy caulkers."* In lxxxiii. 4, &c., of Psalms, Gebal is referred to as one of the confederate nations against Israel. This same Gebal was identical with the place called *Sier*. As we have before shewn, *Sier* in Celtic means *west*, and therefore it may be taken to signify a country or place in the west of Europe. The fact of it being recorded that there were trade communications between Phœnicia and Britain at this early time, goes a great way to prove that the people of Gebal or Sier were inhabitants of South Western Europe.

---

* "O, thou that art situate at the entry of the sea, which art a merchant for the people of many isles."—*Ezek.* xxvii. 3.

The *Gabales* and the Ruteni of Strabo bordered on the Narbonites. In Cæsar's time there were a Gabali under the supremacy of the Arveni and the Helvii, the Swiss of modern Europe.

Again, Strabo tells us that there were silver mines in the countries of the Ruteni and Gabali.

Smith (Classical Dictionary) says "that the Gebalines were the Varduli of Spain."

During the Middle Ages the name Guibelines was applied to one of the opposing factions that kept Europe in anarchy for centuries, called *Guelphs* and *Guibelines*. They were noble and powerful families of Northern Italy—the Viscorili, Doria, Della, Scala, Pelaviconi, were Gebalines.

In Ezekiel xxvii. 3, we have—"O thou that art situated at the entry of the sea which art a merchant for the people of many isles;" from which we suppose it is to be inferred that the people of the Grecian Isles in those days traded with Tyre; but we find in the same chapter, 12th verse, that "Tarshish was thy merchant by reason of the multitude of all kind of riches : with silver, iron, tin, and lead they traded in thy fairs." This Tarshish, as before shewn, was Spain; but it is said by some writers that Tarshish included the British Islands. Tarshish, the son of Javan, and grandson of Japhet, whose descendants are believed by some to, for the most part, inhabit Europe, particularly the British Islands, gave his name to *Tarshish*, as we understand it, in the south and west of Europe, and mentioned in connection with the men of Dedan, and also with the names Dan and Javan, which are to the present day almost exclusively native to the west, south, and north of this continent. Harran and Canah and Eden, which are also found here, are referred to in the 23rd and 24th verses of the last mentioned chapter of Ezekiel, as " thy merchants in all sorts of things." Canna is the name of one of the islands of the Hebrides; and it remains to be accounted for by the sceptical, how the name *Eden*, or *Edin*, became prefixed to *burgh*, as we find it in the name *Edin*burgh, and how that there are other repetitions of it, as names of places in England. One of her rivers is also called Eden.

In Ezekiel xxv. 12, 13, 14, Edom, Teman, and Dedan are threatened with vengeance; the same as prophesied by Amos and Obadiah. This was brought about by the *confederacy* against Jacob. Calish, referring to Teman (p. 597) says, " As to the geographical position of Teman, the Bible offers neither direct nor indirect information, except that it once mentions it in parallelism with the mountains of Paran" (Habakkuk iii. 3). The words are—"God came from Teman, and the Holy One from mount *Paran.*"

The Hebrew Bible account of Esau is that he was "red all over, like a hairy cloak, and they called his name Esau." The *Edom*, understood to mean *red earth*, is believed by some to be equivalent to the word Esau. The Culdees and the Essenians are spoken of in connection with the Gebaline, and both had close relationship to the God Ees. Bryant points this out as a Cuthite radical, denoting light and fire, and one of the titles of the sun—("Ancient Mythology," vol. i. p. 31.) In the Irish the word is also spelled Easga and Eascan, the moon. Whether Esau had divine honour paid to him we cannot tell, but it is as likely as not that this word represents the word Easga, or that the latter is formed from the word Esau, or *Ees*, the God *Ees* of Bryant. It is possible that the prefix to *Ess*enian was originally the same word. Esu, Essian, Oisean, are words significant of the esoteric religion, taught by Pythagoras— the word *esoteric* itself seems to be formed from them.

o

The esoteric religion helped to form the Gebaline or Gaelic system.

According to Higgins, *Gble,* Keble, Gabla mean Cabala, *or tradition of wisdom.* " *Gblm,*" Sir W. Drummond says, "were master masons, who put the finishing strokes to the Temple of Solomon ;" " *stone-squarers,*" they were also called.

There is a very celebrated name in Irish mythology, *Gobban-Saer;* of him Keane says, "—— his name that of a class, not of an individual. . . . Gobban-Saer means the *sacred poet,* or the *Freemason-sage,* one of the *Guabhres, or Cabiri,* such as you have seen him represented on the Tuath-de-Danaan Cross at Clonmacnoise. . . ." He then quotes O'Brien :— "The first name ever given to this body [Freemasons] was *Saer,* which has three significations, firstly, *free;* secondly, *mason;* and thirdly, *son of God.* In no language could these several imports be united but in the original one, *viz.,* the Irish. The Hebrews express only one branch of it by *Aliben,* while the English join together the other two." We may conclude from this, that Esau was at least a sojourner in Ireland, and to the present day there are many places called *Dysarts* there, the etymology of which

Keane gives as Di-Ees-ard, the *high* place of the God *Ees*.

Easroe, the ancient name for Ballyshannon, seems in its form—although in that not so much as in it having been the name of a locality noted for the celebration of the Druidical rites—to be the same as Eas or Esau. Besides the place being distinguished in this way, it was the neighbourhood of the Dalhraide, the Red branch of Ulster, the Orgaill, of whom were the MacDonalls of the Hebrides, descendants of the *Calla Vais*, the MacDougalls, MacAlesters. The " Ruderician," or red people of Ulster, are traced to the Ollam or Aulifi—Hebrew, Aleph (אלּיף), or "Dukes," as before mentioned.

The description of Esau as a red man, would seem to single him out as the progenitor of these people.

CONCLUSION.

MANY old things in nature come new to us, surprise us with their apparent similarities to things we know, and we are led on to imagine all sorts of parallels, correspondencies, and relations, that in the end deceive. So in the foregoing pages we have endeavoured to lay before our readers many old, and no doubt surprising things, but their correspondencies, parallels, and relations we at the sametime hold to have established. Yet, if a few of the particulars touched upon have not had all the support we should have given them, it was mainly owing to our desire to limit the book to its present size, in the hope that if it interested it would not tire. We have chiefly endeavoured to show that the Chaldæan, the Hebrew, and the Celt have sent, or brought down to us, such unmistakeable resemblances, that it is fair to conclude they were the same people originally.

The Arphaxadite Chaldæans were the progenitors of the Hebrew Chaldæans, and differ only in name from the first Gaels.

As there are some allusions in the Irish bardic accounts of Fenius Farsaidh and his disciples to the Gaelic and Hebrew languages, a short epitome of these accounts will not be out of place here.

When the Scotic or Milesian colony arrived in Ireland from Spain, the brother of the leader was Amergin, their poet, and chief brehon or judge. From Amergin until the time of Forchern and his composition, the *Uraicecht* or *Primer of the Bards* in the first century, there are many poets and legislators mentioned in Irish records, but the chief of them probably were the two named. Bollandus (Acta SS., ad 17 Mart., tom 2, in Vit. S. Patr., sect. 4) is not alone in denying that the Irish were a lettered people before the Roman alphabet came in with the Christian missionaries. He has the support of a very good scholar the Rev. Thomas Innes, M.A., in his "Critical Essay on the Ancient Inhabitants of the Northern Parts of Britain or Scotland." But as Dr. O'Donovan truly says: "The question has not been as yet handled on either side with a moderation likely to elicit the truth."

Notwithstanding the ingenious disquisitions of these writers, Innes more especially, it is unfortunate for the cause they advocate, that the world has progressed since their time, and knowledge has increased. We can view the question in our day without despising credulity on one side, and prejudice on the other, for both contribute their portions of truth towards the correct solution of the question. The old Irish writers continually refer to their people having had the use of letters from the earliest times—from the period of the Tuath-da-Danaan, who had several distinguished poets among them. Ogma Mac Elathain, understood to have invented one of the species of virgular characters called Ogham, and who afterwards became the goddess of Poetry, Brigid, daughter of Dagda, often invoked by the poets of subsequent ages, are mentioned ; and we are told when, and by whom the Irish letters were invented. Fenius Farsaidh is repeatedly spoken of as great grandson of Japheth, and king of Scythia, and it is said that in Shinar he formed a school, which became celebrated for the learned men it produced. His assistants, *Gaed-hal* and Iar, with their master, are as frequently referred to as having taught Hebrew, and the other languages that began with the confusion at Babel. Fenius Farsaidh, it seems, returned, .after twenty

years of successful presidency in Shinar, to Scythia,
and appointed Gaedhal president of the schools he
established there. O'Donovan (Irish Grammar, Introduction, p. xxix.), says that "King Fenius then ordered
Gaedhal to arrange and digest the Gaelic languages into
five dialects, the most polished of which was to be named
Bearla Feine, after Fenius himself, while the language
generally was to be named Gaidhelg, from Gaedhal.
Fenius Farsaidh, we are told, reigned over Scythia
for a period of twenty-two years after his return from
the plain of Shinar. He had two sons, Nenual and
Niul, to the elder of whom he bequeathed his kingdom, but the younger nothing but his learning. Niul
for many years continued teaching in the public
schools of Scythia, until the fame of his learning
spread abroad into the neighbouring kingdoms; and
at length Pharaoh Cingcris [Cinchres], king of Egypt,
invited him to his country to instruct the Egyptians in
the various languages and sciences of which he was
master. Niul* set out for Egypt, and Pharaoh was so
pleased with him, that he bestowed upon him the land
called Capaciront, or Capacir, situated near the Red

---

* The chief Milesian families trace their pedigrees to this
royal schoolmaster of Egypt.

Sea, and gave him his daughter Scota in marriage, from which the Milesian Irish were afterwards called *Scoti.* After his marriage, Niul erected public schools at Capaciront, and was there, instructing the Egyptians in the arts and sciences, at the very time that Moses took upon him the command of the children of Israel, 797 years after the Deluge. At this time, Niul had by Scota a son, whom he named Gaedhal, in honour of his friend Gaedhal, son of Eathor, and from him, according to some of our historians, the Irish were called Gaoidhil, and their language Gaoid-heilg. The descendants of this famous schoolmaster, after various adventures by sea and land, emigrating from Egypt to Crete; from Crete to Scythia; from Scythia to Gothia, or Getulia; from Gothia or Getulia to Spain; from Spain to Scythia; from Scythia to Egypt again; from Egypt to Thrace; from Thrace to Gothia; from Gothia to Spain; finally arrived in Ireland under the conduct of two brothers, Heber and Heremon, sons of Milesius, and the twenty-first in descent from Gaedhal, son of Niul.

We are told in the *Uraicecht*, preserved in the Book of Lecan, that the ancient Irish alphabet did not begin with the letters a, b, c, like the Latin, nor with

:a, b, g, like the Greek and Hebrew alphabets, but
with the letters b, l, f, from which it received its
name *Bobel-loth;* or with b, l, n, from which, its
appellation *Beth-luis-nion.* Each of the letters of the
Bobel-loth alphabet took its name from one of the
masters who taught at the great schools under Fenius
Farsaidh, and in the Beth-luis-nion alphabet each
letter was named after some tree, for what reason we
know not."

The following shows the striking similarity of sound
and spelling in the names of the letters of the Bobel-
Loth alphabet, and Hebrew proper names, and their
sounds.

THE BOBEL-LOTH ALPHABET.

b,	b Bobel	t, τ	Talemon
l,	l Loth	c, c	Cai
f,	ϝ Foroun	q, q	Qualep
s,	ϒ Saliath	m, ɱ	Mareth
n,	ɳ Nabgadon	g, ɜ	Gath
h,	ɦ Hirwath, or Uria	ng,ɳɜ	Ngoimer
d,	ꝺ Davith	sd,ϒꝺ	Stru
r,	ɭ Ruben	eu, ɛʉ	Iachim or Iumelchus
a,	ᴀ Achab	oi, oȷ	Ordinos
o,	o Ose	ui, ʉȷ	Judæmos
u,	ʉ Uriath	io, ȷo	Jodonius
i,	ȷ Etrocuis, or Esu	a, ᴀ́	Aifrin

The reader will bear in mind what is said of Fenius Farsaidh having taught Hebrew, and he can then have little difficulty in admitting that the balance of probability, if not of truth, is on the side, that, his schoolmasters, from their names, were Hebrew; which, if granted, must, from the evidence we have brought to bear upon the affinity of the Celtic and Hebrew languages and people, lead to the conclusion that they were of the same original.

In the *Beth-luis-nion* alphabet there are some remarkable resemblances to the sounds of the Hebrew and Greek letters, thus :—

Hebrew.	Greek.	Irish.	
B	ב beth	B beta	B bejc	beith, beech-tree.
N	נ nun	N nu	N ηjoη	nion, ash-tree.
R	ר resh	P rho	R ʀuјr	ruis, bore-tree-elder.
A	א aleph	A alpha	ᴀ ᴅjlɪη	ailm, palm-tree.
E	ה he	H eta	e eᴅᴅᴅ	eadhadh, aspen.

The system of letters of the Chaldæans, the Hebrews, the Greeks, and the Celts, must have been originally the same. Mr. Huddleston says upon this point : "If the Irish had culled or selected their alphabet from that of the Romans, as some persons have absurdly imagined, how, or by what miracle could they have hit on the identical letters which Cadmus brought from Phœnicia and rejected all the rest?"

Mr. Astle argues that the Phœnician alphabet was the origin of the " Hebrew or Samaritan, the Chaldaic, the Bastulan, the Punic Carthaginian or Sicilian, the Pelasgian Greek;" and Higgins in his Anacalypsis observes that the Arabic—to which we have made frequent references—"Was a language before the present Hebrew, Greek, Sanskrit, and *Deva-Negari* letters were invented."*

SUGGESTIVE EXPLANATION OF SOME OF THE BOBEL-
LOTH LETTERS.

Bobel seems to initiate *language*, or to commemorate the confusion of speech, and may be repre- sented by the word *Babel*, which has a like significance. It is not a little wonderful how the word *babble* has come down to us, signifying to talk *confusedly*.

Saliath, according to Forchern's spelling (or *Salia*,

* "Preliminary Observations," cap. I. p. 16.

Vallancey), seems to be intended for *Salah*, the son of Arphaxad, who, if we allow, as suggested elsewhere, to be the same as *Farsaidh* (Fenius), there is not much to hinder us believing that his son became a teacher on the plain of Shinar, as contended for in Europe.

Davith is unquestionably to be understood as David—*a* David—we do not consider that the first of the name was the son of Jesse.

Gath (or *Gad*,—the *th* is often used in old Irish writings substituted for *d*), *Gad* was the name of one of the sons of Jacob.

Vgomer, the name of the eldest son of Japhet was most likely bestowed upon one of Farsaidh's schoolmasters.

Ruben, one of the sons of Jacob was called by this name.

Ose, perhaps the genitive of the name Hosea, one of the prophets.

Etrocuis, or *Esu* (according to Forchern, *Etro*, and the Book of Lecan, *Ur*),—*Esu* seems to be so like the word Esau that in order to

avoid the possibility of the ill-natured charging
us with philological lunacy or something like
it, we will not comment upon it, but leave it
to the judgment of the reader.

Judæmos,—the affix of this word has a Greco-
Latin appearance, but if divested of it, there
is much likelihood that we have the origin
of the word Judah.

These names, in their similarities, are to be
accounted for in one or two other ways beside the
above. Some one might say the Irish had them
from the Hebrews, and no doubt they would feel
quite satisfied assuming this an explanation; but
how get over the difficulty of the old Druidical and
Chaldæan rites, their traditions, the multiplicity of
Jewish names of people and places, in the west of
Europe, that withstood the shock of time, even before
the advent of our Lord, and have survived to the
present with stubborn adherence to the inhabitants
and to the soil of these islands? Let this be answered by those only who have studied both sides
of the question, they only are competent to answer
correctly, or at least reasonably. The fact of so

many letters in the Bobel-loth alphabet having significance of Hebrew sounds and proper names,—names
recognisable in the early history of the Hebrew,
proves the close relationship they held to the first
Celtic peoples,* who have preserved these names likewise; both had them from the same immediate source,
and possibly they were originally one people, inhabiting the same country, and enjoying the same laws and
institutions. Their similarity, even as we know them
in the present day, is apparent, alike to Jew and Celt.
The Celt, like the Hebrew, has from time immemorial,
obeyed the ubiquitous instinct of his nature, and gone
hither and thither over the world. For centuries before
the Christian period he is found wandering over the
earth, and in the nineteenth century his nature is as
unchanged as the Hebrew. Dispersed over thousands
of miles, and, separated in place, as well as in time, they
have lost their original race identity, and, even at this

* "In the *Morning Herald* for the 16th or 17th of April 1827,
is a paragraph, stating that the Bible Societies were giving
Hebrew Bibles to the native Irish, as it was found that they
were better understood than the English. This, in a very
remarkable manner, supports what Col. Vallancey has main-
tained, but which has been much ridiculed by weak people, that
Ireland was colonized by a tribe from the East, and particularly
from Phœnicia."—Note from Higgin's Anacalypsis, p. 443.

hour, are only beginning to catch glimpses of their pre-historic oneness.

The sooner philologists and inquirers after truth direct their studies above the prejudice of school and university, the sooner the Celtic tongue and archæology will be acknowledged to claim their close attention ; the sooner too will biblical students find their way out of the labyrinth of contradictory interpretations by which they are enclosed, and walk in a purer and clearer atmosphere of research.

THE END.

STEVENS AND RICHARDSON, PRINTERS, 5, GREAT QUEEN STREET, W.C.